presents

THE LADYBALLER'S GUIDE TO LIFE

SoccerGrlProbs

Carly Beyar, Shannon Fay, and Alanna Locast

TRIUMPH
BOOKS

Library of Congress Cataloging-in-Publication Data available upon request.

This book is available in quantity at special discounts for your group or organization. For further information, contact:

Triumph Books LLC
814 North Franklin Street
Chicago, Illinois 60610
(312) 337-0747
www.triumphbooks.com

Printed in U.S.A.
ISBN: 978-1-62937-770-4
Design by Patricia Frey

Photos courtesy of SoccerGrlProbs unless otherwise indicated

To all the soccer girls reading this: trust us when we say that even though soccer may be the most frustrating thing in your life at times, the good moments will always, always outweigh the bad. You will build lifelong relationships with your teammates, grow in self-confidence and inner pride, and create memories that will make up tenfold for that time you got benched for making a simple mistake or that party you missed because you were traveling for a game. You only get one soccer career. Make the most of it, and enjoy every second of it!

To our families, for shaping us into the strong, confident, and proud women we are today.

Contents

Foreword

How is just being ourselves so challenging? I mean, how is it there are so many things that can interrupt the process of us feeling good and finding our true north? The challenges are many, and this is why *The Ladyballer's Guide to Life* is a fantastic resource to navigate the obstacles that people, time, school, recruiting, sports, and extracurriculars may throw our way.

When I look back at my younger self, I could have used some guidance from women who knew what it was like. Now, there are plenty of resources that young women can use to help them, but this book is unique. It's told in real language, with real examples of challenges that will help you see things more clearly.

One, know you are **not alone**. This would have been helpful for me to know, as I had two ACL reconstructions—yes, two—in the first three years of my college career. I had *no idea* what to expect nor how to navigate the journey ahead.

Two, I was a transfer student, so assimilating into a new environment, culture, and friend groups proved challenging.

Three, I was a **competitive beast** who just wanted to play, and sometimes that rubbed people the wrong way. I could have used words of wisdom to help articulate my feelings, needs, or ideas, but instead they stayed bottled up.

My Ladyballers Carly, Alanna, and Shannon have created a vehicle for positive change and assistance as you meander, jog, trot, sprint, or explode down your life's path. Use the wisdom shared as your history to your new future. **Be well. Stay resolute.** And always look to **be inspired.**

—Brandi Chastain, your No. 6

Brandi Chastain is a two-time FIFA Women's World Cup champion, two-time Olympic gold medalist, coach, and sports broadcaster. She played for the United States national team from 1988 to 2004 and was inducted into the National Soccer Hall of Fame in March 2017.

Chapter One

WELCOME TO THE CLUB, LADYBALLER

Welcome to *The Ladyballer's Guide to Life*, written to help you through the roller-coaster ride that is being a collegiate soccer player. Meet your new best friends: Carly Beyar, Shannon Fay, and Alanna Locast, three former NCAA Division I student-athletes and the creators of @SoccerGrlProbs. We're here to help you master the Dos & Don'ts of playing college soccer, balancing your sport, academic, and social life, as well as creating a healthy body and mindset, staying motivated, and being the best you that you can be. There is an art to remaining sane while playing the beautiful game. Take it from players who have been through it all.

The purpose of this book is for the three of us to share with you our "Ladyballer Nuggets of Wisdom" in the hopes that you can use this guide to become the most epic Ladyballer you can be. But wait; we should probably explain what a Ladyballer is first:

Ladyballer (lay-DEE-bawl-er) (*noun*): A rare breed of awesome female who has an incredible passion for the game, a wardrobe consisting of tournament T-shirts, and an appetite fit for a hippopotamus.

This is a term you'll hear us use when speaking highly of another female athlete. Let's be honest; we all strive to be a Ladyballer. She is chill and fun to be around. Her favorite movie is *She's the Man* and her favorite parties involve pasta. Her hair is perpetually knotted in a ponytail and/ or giant pineapple bun on top of her head, and you can bet your bottom dollar that an abundance of hair ties adorns her wrist. A thigh gap is most definitely the last thing on her mind as she surrendered to the struggle of skinny jeans years ago. She loves her toned muscles and is comfortable in her own skin—with or without makeup. Not only does she value commitment, time management, communication skills, and leadership, she's also a team player with an insatiable thirst for progress, on and off the field. She's a boss, in all facets of life. Oh, and she follows @SoccerGrlProbs religiously, watches all their videos, and tells all her friends about them. 😌

Our story began at Fairfield University, where the three of us met in preseason as Division I athletes on the women's soccer team. Between our second and third training sessions of the day (also known as *three-a-days*) during the preseason of August 2011, we found ourselves venting about all the absurd moments and frustrating problems we were experiencing. We kept laughing at how funny we thought we were (because that's what you do with your team...hysterically laugh about the nonsense that no one else would even understand), and with that came the spontaneous birth of our Twitter handle, @SoccerGrlProbs. We now had a comedic outlet to all share our inner thoughts and the funny moments that make up a female athlete's everyday life.

It's no secret how crazily intertwined the soccer community is. Our teammates told their high school teammates, club teammates, friends, and coaches about the Twitter handle, and within weeks our following had grown to hundreds. We couldn't believe how fast it had taken off. We vowed that when

we hit 1,000 followers we would streak down the library hill—
until the moment we hit 1,000 followers. We quickly changed
the "streaking number" to 20,000. When we hit 20,000,
it became 100,000. Then once we hit 100,000, it became
200,000. And ever since then, we've been avoiding that library
hill like the plague.

Little did we know that we had struck a chord with young
women just like us across the country, who wanted more
content they could relate to. So we said, "Why not?" We
frolicked around campus, giggling at ourselves, armed with
an iPad and a soccer ball, capturing the ridiculous moments
that filled our everyday lives. This was no fancy film crew; we
were essentially just friends and teammates, reenacting the
daily shenanigans female soccer players stumble through:
struggling to get up the stairs after a tough conditioning
practice, sporting bruises and turf burns all over our legs
during summer, eating an extra slice of pizza without a worry
because we know we'll "run it off later." Picture us, three
athletes with an iPad reenacting or saying something weird

PHOTO CREDIT: Daphne Youree

and being overheard by someone on campus. We specifically remember one time we were filming in the cafeteria at school and the employees were giving us weird looks, no doubt thinking to themselves, *What the heck are you doing?* We would always get the scene done as fast as possible and then laugh hysterically as we sprinted to the next filming location.

In February 2012, we created and posted our first video, "Sh*t Soccer Girls Say." We noticed about an hour after we put the video out that there were only 306 views. How could that be? It was stuck on that number for hours! We thought we uploaded the video wrong (because chances were…we did). The next morning, we woke up and refreshed the YouTube page. The number didn't say 306 anymore. It now said more than 1 million views! Cue the jaw drop; we were flabbergasted. We had everyone and their mother (we mean this literally) calling us to tell us that they saw us in "that new soccer video!" What had originally been created as a venting outlet for our team had grown into so much more. Our fans asked us for T-shirts with funny lines from our YouTube videos and tweets, so we made a cheap, simplistic website. We're still not sure how people trusted it enough to input their credit card information; it looked very sketchy! We created three T-shirts, each with a funny line, put them up on the website, and we sold out! All 300 T-shirts were gone in few hours. In fact, we forgot to set an inventory limit, because we didn't think we'd sell more than 10 T-shirts. We're laughing now, but that was probably not a good idea because we didn't even physically have the shirts yet. Oops! Lo and behold, the number of orders kept crawling in. What had we gotten ourselves into? Or even better, how did we get *this* lucky!?

Keep in mind, we were three non-business majors, two of whom were still playing college soccer, trying to navigate the ins and outs of starting a business. When our YouTube video went viral and our Twitter account blew up, people started

to notice us more. During in-season games, our opponents would recognize us on the field and say, "Wait, I know you; aren't you one of the girls from that video?" In one instance, we heard the fans playing our "Sh*t Soccer Girls Say" video on the sideline during the game! We wanted to remain anonymous until we graduated, but what are you going to do? People recognized our faces!

We knew we were part of something special. We had found a one-of-a-kind niche of amazing and loyal fans with a need we were fulfilling. We were simultaneously surprised and proud to hear from fans and parents that we were empowering young female athletes simply by authentically being ourselves. Fast forward a few years. We graduated from Fairfield University and joined their entrepreneurship program. This program was a game-changer for us. They provided us with professors and mentors from the alumni community who helped us understand how to run and monetize our business. (Fistbump to Chris, Michael, and Teddy. We cannot thank you enough.) We commonly asked questions like, "What the heck is a mission statement? *And what is ours?*" "How do state taxes work?" "What's a domain?" It was definitely a learning experience, but it paid off big time.

We loved being able to stay local after graduating. In fact, all three of us moved in together near Fairfield Beach! Picture our neighborhood, a gorgeous residential road with massive beach houses and pristine cut lawns. Yeah...we weren't living in those houses. We had the tiny shack that was sandwiched between $2 million mansions...but it worked for us! All we needed was a garage for our inventory, a fridge big enough for our appetites, and at least three bedrooms for the sake of our sanity. We were teammates, coworkers, and now roomies... let the fun begin. It's true, we never had an "off" button and constantly felt like we were working, but laughing hysterically every day, putting out hilarious YouTube and social content constantly, and shipping our apparel right from the comfort of our own living room couch wasn't so bad after all. We had so much fun...aside from cutting the lawn and paying rent. That was the worst!

As the months went on, we continued to work extremely hard to establish ourselves and our company in the soccer community. We joined Davidson College's Next Play Venture Pitch Tournament and won $8,000 as the only women in the competition. We traveled to countless tournaments and set up our T-shirt and apparel table in the freezing fall and winter months to help get face time with our fans. (No, not Facetime video chatting; actually meeting fans IRL.) The big turning point was in May of 2015. We received an email from a company called COPA90 wanting to chat about the 2015 Women's World Cup. We said, "Sure, no problem," but wondered what the heck they wanted to chat about. While on the conference call, we heard KickTV's head of content, Jimmy Conrad, say, "We want to pay you as correspondents to follow Team USA and cover the World Cup in Canada for the entire month of June." Our jaws dropped. *Holy cow! Holy moly!* "Oh yes, hold on one moment," we said, as we put the call on mute so that we could quickly scream with happiness. Trying to keep our cool, we took them off mute and said, 'Yes, yes, a resounding yes.' This trip changed our company forever.

With Team USA winning the 2015 World Cup, people in the country were starting to take women's soccer more seriously! There was an increase in awareness and attention to the women's sport, and we wanted to keep that momentum going. We ultimately wanted to support and grow the women's game in any way we could. Cue an uptick in our social media posts promoting games, blogs recapping big tournaments, and female empowerment shirts in the store. Brands started to notice our shift from "just funny" to "funny and empowering."

For the next few years, we worked with brands that were devoting their energy to continuing the momentum in women's soccer like Nike, Adidas, and Puma. We even got to partner with Nike on an apparel collaboration! We talked at as many camps and traveled to as many clubs around the country as we could about the college recruiting process and balancing the student-athlete life, which helped us feel even more connected with our following. We also got to work with six of the NWSL teams to continue to promote and support the league and the players as the momentum of women's soccer continued to build!

Then Adidas knocked on our door to send us to the 2019 World Cup in France! We were so excited to be onsite at every single USA game. We had the opportunity to use our large platform as a voice to promote the women's soccer games and highlights with our own authentic spin.

To date, we have produced more than 120 videos on YouTube and accumulated more than 37 million views and 55 million minutes watched (and counting). Our online shop that started with just three simple shirts now has more than 100 soccer-related products. To say we love going to work every day is an understatement. What's not to love about filming funny soccer videos, continuing to promote the beautiful game we love and, most importantly, wearing sweats to the office? We truly believe, whether it's in a big or small way, that we can help

CREDIT: Keara Russell

17

change the game for Ladyballers everywhere and redefine what it means to be a badass, confident female athlete.

SoccerGrlProbs isn't just a social media channel that puts out funny videos, relatable tweets, and hilarious Instagram memes (although, admittedly, we do pride ourselves on that). We are a business that aims to help the modern female athlete; the girl rocking sweatpants with her hair up to class because she just came from practice, the muscular girl who wouldn't dare trade her strength to fit in differently sized clothing, the girl who can't go to prom because she "has soccer."

We're talking about **you**. You aren't like everyone. We know you are #NotYourAverageGirl. That's why our mission is to support and encourage the well-being and positive self-image of young female athletes everywhere. We want to empower you to build a strong inner foundation. We want you to have the pride and confidence to grow into an independent, motivated, and successful woman. We want to continue to deliver authentic and original content through our brand as a means to establish a sense of unity and sisterhood in the female soccer community. Anyway, enough about us! We are going to prep you to be the best person, friend, daughter, and student-athlete you can be by spilling our Dos & Don'ts of playing soccer. You are our new, beloved bestie, to whom we're going to tell our most helpful secrets.

Chapter Two

TRYOUTS AND PRESEASON

Preseason (*noun*): An excessively sweaty period of two to four weeks when athletes cut their summers short to reunite for rigorous training workouts and whole new levels of soreness and hunger they didn't think were possible. One may experience pressure to get into the most fit and technical shape possible leading into the regular season. Players call it "Hell on Earth, with a Side of Pasta Parties." Coaches call it "The Most Wonderful Time of the Year."

So you decided to try out for a team. Congrats! Maybe this is a team you are returning to, or maybe you're trying out for the first time. Either way, you already got past the hardest part, which was taking the plunge to try out for a team! It takes balls (soccer balls, of course) to put yourself out there in an unfamiliar new situation, so you should be proud of yourself. You've got nothing to lose now. Just think; this could be the start of meeting a new and amazing soccer family who pushes you, motivates you, and supports you! Three things are crucial to help you make it through your tryouts and preseason: **preparation**, **training**, and your **mindset**. What will you do when you're on your own trying to prepare leading up to your tryouts? How will you train yourself? And how will you build your mindset to be one that is constantly feeding you positivity?

Preseason is a time of mixed feelings, of being beyond pumped for the season to start up again but so anxious and nervous about all of the unknowns to come. We all look forward to games and training as a team and pasta parties, but the unfamiliar feeling of new players on the team, fighting for a spot, and not knowing what fitness tests will be thrown at you or how you will perform are all things that contribute to the preseason scaries. There are, however, some things you can be *sure* of. You know you're going to be very sore. You'll probably have some nagging blisters from not playing in cleats this often. Everyone will be a little on edge because you are all fighting for a starting spot. However, what's most important to focus on to get you through tryouts and preseason is all the good that will come along with it. It's a reunion between you and a bunch of your friends or a new beginning with a ton of incredible new friends. You're getting in awesome shape, and you're setting the foundation for what hopes to be an undefeated season!

Preparation Dos

- **Summer training is crucial for college soccer players.**
  Not only is the offseason spectacularly short, but
  preseason occurs in the hottest, most brutal month known
  to womankind. The summer is your time to make sure you
  survive preseason. Remember that every time you want
  to cancel a training session, finish a weightlifting session
  early, cut short your run, ignore your technical work...there's
  an opponent (or even a teammate) who refuses to quit.

- **Look over the fitness packet that your conditioning
  coach sent your way.** Even if it isn't mandatory, use it
  as guidance to familiarize yourself with the workouts and
  exercises. If you haven't been given a fitness packet, ask
  the coach, conditioning coach, or older teammates for
  recommendations to get preseason-ready. Get those
  fitness sessions going, girl, especially in the weight room.
  Freshman year preseason will be *much* less of a shock to

your body if you are prepared. Plus, practice and games are always more fun when you can breathe.

> ■ Shannon went up to Fairfield to train with the conditioning coach prior to preseason and had him recommend a strength and conditioning coach on Long Island whom she trained with the year before going to college. She felt confident and educated in the weight room and was able to skip the additional I've-never-lifted-before soreness.

- **Come into preseason ready to pass fitness tests.** There should be no surprises here. If you're lucky, you'll know ahead of time what those tests are and what numbers will be considered passing. If you find yourself having a hard time training alone, grab a teammate or a friend (or even your mom) and ask them to time you or join you during your workouts. The best thing about playing the most popular sport on the planet is that you're never alone.

- **Break in those new cleats before you go.** Play in them, run in them, wear them everywhere. It's not like you're saving your new white sneakers for the first day of school. Literally do anything—even shower in them; we promise it works. (Just don't walk around on the hardwood floors; otherwise, Mom will be pissed!) If you open that cleat box on day one of preseason, you'll most likely shred your feet with blisters by forcing them in cleats for six-plus hours a day. Do. Not. Ignore. This. Tip.

- **Work out early in the morning and/or later in the evening because of the heat.** Take care of your body before and, more importantly, after training: hydrate, roll

SoccerGirlProblems® @SoccerGrlProbs · Aug 25
You know you're in preseason when going down the stairs hurts just as much as going up them #FeelTheBurn #SGP

out, stretch, and put your legs up. Trust us, your body will thank you.

- **Get creative on vacation: beach runs, swimming, frisbee, hiking.** We know it's your summer. Of course you can and should relax with your family. Just be sure not to let it distract you completely from what you've been working so hard for. Do whatever you can to stay active when away from your normal routine.

- **Keep playing on a team, if your area has one.** Spend time getting touches on the ball or go down to the field nearby and find a pick-up game. There are even apps for this! If all else fails, who says you can't take a bunch of balls and cones to the local high school turf and work on an aspect of your game by yourself?

- **Listen to your body and give yourself rest.** Rest is one of the most undervalued aspects of an athlete's life. We are wired to push ourselves and test our limits at all costs. However, this often means we play through pain and soreness, to the point of doing more harm than good. Too much pain or soreness can be signs that you might be overtraining. If you have a nagging injury or feel like you got a subpar night's sleep, sometimes a day of rest is the *best* thing you can do for your training. It will allow you to come back fully charged for a purposeful workout.

Preparation Don'ts

- **Don't lose sight of your goals.** We understand it's summertime and you're in relaxation nation, but you have made a commitment! That doesn't mean you can't be involved in fun activities and relaxation. Just make sure you remember that every amount of backward progress you do to your body today will be something you'll have to make up for tomorrow.

- **Don't make excuses.** If there is one thing coaches don't want to hear, it's that you "didn't have time" to prep for preseason, or that you are suddenly "injured." There isn't a faster way for a coach to lose respect for you than by coming into preseason unprepared or with excuses. If you're truly passionate about playing college soccer, you will do what is expected of you. Few things in life compare to being part of something bigger than yourself like being on a college soccer team. When you prepare yourself mentally and physically, preseason isn't so torturous anymore. You will excel and exceed expectations, and guess what? If you adequately prepare and stay motivated, you may even have a starting position as a freshman. Get. It. Girl. Thank us later.

- **Don't skip lifting.** All college players should receive a summer training packet, and that packet will include several lifts among various running workouts. Don't skip these! You may think you can hide from the weights, but they will hit you *hard* if you try and avoid them, and create an easy way to be singled out by your strength and conditioning coach. Lifting is part of being a Ladyballer. The point of lifting in our sport is not to make you bulky or thick. The goal is to get *stronger.* You will do enough cardio and sprints while playing soccer to remain a lean, mean, soccer machine. Plus, the right kind of lifting will reduce your risk for injury, and who doesn't want that? The moral of the story: you can't be in your best shape and be the best Ladyballer you can be without strength training.

  - In Carly's experience, she was totally intimidated by the freshmen fitness packet. She figured if she did just the running side of things, she'd be fine during preseason. Little did she know, this was a terrible idea! Walking into the weight room and doing strength testing was hard. She couldn't even lift the bar by herself! Learn from our past experiences.

- **Don't bother overpacking.** Chances are you will stop caring about dressing up by day three. (Or you'll at least realize you don't have the energy to keep that up all preseason.) Just own it; rock those T-shirts and sweats. Throw your hair up. Be a sweaty mess. Embrace it.

SoccerGirlProblems®
@SoccerGrlProbs

How shaving around turf burn feels...
#SoccerGrlProbs

Training Dos

- **When you're on the field, make sure to train as hard as possible.** Preseason is filled with borderline scorching temperatures, turf burns, horrific tan lines, and never-ending frustration. But guess what? You're surrounded by two dozen or so teammates going through the same thing you are. Coach is watching you and wants to know, *Who is going to help this team succeed? Who will be my starting 11? Who can I rely on?* Don't stop working hard. It'll all be worth it when the season starts.

- **Expect multiple practices.** There will be two-a-days and maybe even three-a-days, including conditioning, strength training, scrimmaging, or some technical work. You will most likely begin and end your day on the field. Stay alert and sharp so you are ready to go throughout the day.

- **For the love of Alex Morgan, bring a fan.** We can't stress enough how important this is. Air-conditioned dorms in preseason are rare, if not a complete farce. If you have them, congrats; and we're jealous. This is most likely where you and your team will be setting up camp for preseason.

- **Rest in between sessions!** The schedule is rigorous, and you should thank your body for working so hard by letting it truly rest during downtime and get a good night's sleep. Sleep is an integral part of being a competitive athlete. This will give you the highest odds to perform your best during training and impress Coach. You may try to start off preseason watching movies until midnight with your teammates and hanging out in the cafeteria after lunch with the men's team, but your body will quickly let you know that an early bedtime is what it wants and needs. Don't fight it. #WheresMyBlankie

- **Pick each other up during training sessions, both literally and mentally.** If you knock someone down, help them up. If you see someone is mentally down on themselves, help them up, too. Everyone's busting their asses, everyone's tense, and everyone's one mess-up away from crying. Be a positive force on your team during training, and someone will return the favor to you when you need it.

CREDIT: Hannah Clayton

- **Take care of your blisters and cuts.** Odds are, you're bound to get one or two. These nasty little suckers can get infected *really* easily when your feet are in and out of cleats all day long. We've had teammates literally miss practices until their feet healed. Sounds kinda sissy, doesn't it? Don't let this happen to you.

- **Keep your toenails short.** This will save you a whole lot of pain and you'll get to skip the experience of only having 8 out of 10 toenails from getting stepped on.

- **Try your hardest.** This almost goes without saying. Being a student-athlete is a privilege; you only get this opportunity for four years. Understand that continued effort yields success, on and off the field. Are we right or are we right?

Training Don'ts

- **Don't complain or vent out loud at training, especially within earshot of Coach.** No "I'm so tired," "I hate this," or "this sucks." This attitude and those complaints are like poison to a team. Teams thrive on positive mentalities, not Negative Nancies. Keep your head up and call Mom or your BFF from home afterward to explain how ridiculously tired you are after those 100s. Venting in private keeps you sane, without giving anyone on your team a negative feeling. Remember, there's always something to be gained from your struggles. Those 100-yard sprints after practice that have your legs feeling like jelly are exactly what will keep your engine running when you're in double overtime against a top 25 team. Practice good mental habits.

- **Don't undermine your coach's training sessions.** It doesn't matter how pointless you think a drill is; keep it to yourself. Be coachable and adapt to the team's style of play

and goals. Your preseason and regular season will be that much more enjoyable if you can learn how to be cohesive with the team and commit to making the most of every training session.

- **Don't half-ass anything.** Whatever you do, always use your full ass.

Mindset Dos

- **Have a positive mindset from the beginning of the season to the end.** Positivity is contagious and the feeling will spread throughout your team. If your team reacts positively after a loss or encourages each other after hard fitness sessions, everyone's mentality will be resilient and your team will bounce back faster. Keep your eyes on the prize and your head in place and you'll be hoisting the championship hardware while simultaneously dumping Gatorade on your coaches' heads come season's end.

- **Encourage others.** It's easy to tell when someone is struggling to get through something. Throw a few words of encouragement their way or even a nice text message. It doesn't have to be some *Rocky* monologue before the big fight. It can be as simple as "you've got this" or "just breathe," and it might be exactly what they need to hear. You've got nothing to lose by encouraging others. We've also found that sending inspirational video links works wonders, too!

- **Be coachable.** It doesn't matter if you've got the hardest shot, or the best technical footwork, or invincible speed. If you're not coachable, there's not much progress to be made. Being coachable will greatly increase your odds of getting playing time and making a big impact!

- **Have fun!** This is the point we often forget. The whole reason you play this game is because you love it and it brings you joy! Just because preseason is a stressful and high-strung time of the season, don't let it ruin your love for soccer.

Mindset Don'ts

- **Don't give up.** No matter how tough it gets, or how worried you are that you can't keep up, just don't quit. Everyone had to go through their first preseason, and odds are it sucked for every single one of your teammates. Remember, you are at preseason to get better; and you will! Don't give up before the hard work has had a chance to pay off.

- **Don't get stuck on *one* mistake.** This is the unfortunate downfall of most athletes. They'll miss an open-netter,

get nutmegged on defense, or let in an easy goal, and then it's all downhill from there. They keep replaying that same mistake over and over in their head for the rest of the practice. They're so focused on the negative that they never get the chance to redeem themselves. Don't get down on yourself. (We know, this is easier said than done!)

- When Carly was younger, she remembers scrimmaging at tryouts and losing the ball to a forward. Her first reaction was to do everything in her power to win the ball back, and so she did. At the end of the tryout, the coach pulled her aside and said they noticed how hard she worked to get the ball back in possession and for that reason, she made the team! That goes to show you that the coach is not "out to get you" or looking to highlight your mistakes. They want to see how you react to them! Shake it off, forget it even happened, and stay focused on what you have to do next. Trust us, this will be much more productive than beating yourself up.

- **Don't hold back!** Tryouts and preseason are the time to show your coach what you've got. You don't want the week to be over and be left thinking to yourself, *Ugh, I wish I would have left it all on the field.* So take the risks, try the move you've been working on, take advantage of the shooting opportunity, make a dive for the ball you don't think you stand a chance of saving. Now is the time to give it your all. What do you have to lose?

Chapter Three

FITNESS TESTING

Fitness Testing (*noun*): The act of running as fast and lifting as much as you possibly can while trying not to cry under the magnifying glass of coaches assessing how fit and capable you are as a runner, player, and human being.

Let's face it, fitness tests are an unavoidable (and somewhat necessary) part of being a soccer player. Physical limitations impede skill acquisition, so most, if not all coaches prefer that you come into season in good shape. When a team comes into season in good shape, it makes it much easier for the coach to focus on individual skills as well as collective team skill sets.

Now, every coach's definition of "good shape" is a little different; some may realistically look for some timed 120s or a 7:30 minute mile. Others may set standards that seem on par with Olympic track and field benchmarks that you may just die in the process of trying to achieve. So what exactly is it about fitness testing that makes every soccer player shudder at the thought of it? It seems whether we are prepared or not we all feel a wave of nervousness and anxiety when it comes time to test. Perhaps we all feed off each other's hysteria as we're lined up on the end line waiting to hear Coach's whistle accompanied with a *ya gotta move!*

If you're new to fitness tests, here are some of the most popular ones you may run into during your soccer days;

Timed Mile: There's just something about running four times around a track as fast as you can while trying not to pee your pants that haunts you forever.

Timed 2 Mile: Double the feelings above from the timed mile, and your coach is double the crazy. You want me to do a six-minute mile *twice*? Get outta here!

Beep or Yo-Yo Test: This test is a whole bunch of running back and forth in 20- to 25-yard increments at the sound of a beep for as long as you possibly can. Sounds joyous, right? You'll be hearing beeps in your nightmares from this one.

ManU Test: This one involves the length of a soccer field. The coach usually gives you *x* amount of time to sprint down and you have the remainder of the minute to jog back to where you started. Gross, we know. Depending on your coach's level of evil, you may do anywhere from 10 to 20 of these.

Perimeters: Just as gross as laps around a track, but a little more comforting that it's on a soccer field.

300s: We can't even.

Other tests you might encounter: Vertical jump, broad jump, sit & reach, and more. These tests are usually not as important as getting playing time, but they are a huge indicator of your explosive power. They are also a great measurement to gather starting-point data so that by the end of the season you can see how much you've improved when you retest.

We want you to know that it's *okay* to feel anxiety over fitness tests and that you are most definitely not alone if the words "beep test" trigger you to curl up in the fetal position. It's important to know that even though fitness tests often result in a number or time score, a coach often holds these tests to learn about you *mentally*; a sort of test of will to see if you are capable of digging deep and giving your best effort and if you're encouraging and cheering your teammates on to do their best too. So as important it is to try and pass these tests,

CREDIT: Hannah Clayton

it's also very important to show your coach a valiant effort and positive mindset!

One huge benefit of these fitness tests is that your team most likely *will* bond over these memories and be brought closer together by your mutual suffering. You *will* come out on the other side mentally stronger and with a sense of accomplishment for having made it through. Here are our Dos and Don'ts to help you make the most of it.

Fitness Test Dos

- **Just. Do. It.** Don't go through the motions because you're too busy sulking that Coach made the team do a surprise beep test during the season (our deepest condolences). You're fit, and you know this will only make your team better. Go out there and work as hard as you can every chance you get. Even if you don't do well that day, your coach can discern between the hard workers and the slugs. The girl working her ass off to barely make the 10th 100-yard sprint by the skin of her teeth speaks volumes more than the girl who easily got to 10 reps and then stopped because that was all she needed to pass. And trust us, you'll feel even worse if a lazy day or session earns your tush a one-way ticket to the bench. Slacking when others are hustling is a no-no. Push through the short-term pain and it'll be worth it in the long-term.

- **Pee *before* fitness testing starts.** Even if you think you don't have to, just try. We know, we sound like overly concerned moms, but trust us. We've witnessed many timed miles that ended in pee-soaked shorts. And yes, even though it's a judgment-free zone, nobody has fun peeing their pants and gasping for air at the same time.

- **Be a leader by example.** Sometimes you don't even need to mutter one word to inspire others around you. Do what you're expected to and be the best you can be while doing it. You'll make yourself and your teammates better because of it.

- **Wear a good running shoe!** We can't emphasize this enough. If your team is not provided a running and training shoe, go to your local running store and get fitted by a professional. They might even have a 3D scanner that you can step on and get immediate recommendations that make sense for your foot type (overpronated, underpronated, your gait, etc.). Make sure to choose a sneaker that will support you both during running and training in the weight room. You'll be more comfortable and perform better!

- **Keep changing your planting leg.** If you're running a fitness test that involves a lot of pivoting and change of direction, such as a shuttle run where you have to run back and forth between two lines, keep alternating the leg that you are turning on. It may help save that one leg from fatiguing early.

- **Think about strength.** Depending on what level you are playing at or what age you are, you may have strength tests like bench presses, squats, push-ups, and more. This is where your preseason strength training comes into play! This will also be your "base" level for the season. So make sure you don't neglect your strength because you are so focused on running. It is also important to note that strength contributes to speed and power, too!

Fitness Test Don'ts

- **Don't tell yourself,** *I can't do it!* A positive mindset is 100 percent necessary. If you believe you can, then you will!

- **Don't cheat yourself.** Stop faking an injury and instead, get on the line with the rest of your teammates. No one likes the girl who conveniently needs to go to the trainer right as fitness testing is supposed to start (and this is usually a repeat offender). On the other hand, if you are actually injured, then you are putting yourself at risk by participating in the fitness test, so be smart about it. Unspoken rule: if you were able to do the entire practice just fine, you're probably fine to do the conditioning at the end, too.

- **Don't be the one who cuts corners during perimeters and field loops.** That doesn't fly in college. Everyone will know you did it. (That corner cone didn't just knock itself over.) Not to mention, your teammates are likely to shower you with dirty looks if the whole team has to repeat the drill because of you! If you're instructed to sprint to the line and

back...*touch the line*. Skipping those three inches is not making you any better.

- **Don't complain...out loud.** Trust us, all we ever wanted to do was complain about the living hell we were about to go through, but it will only create negative vibes. And let us tell you, those bad vibes are *infectious* and can poison the team mentality. You want to be part of creating a more supportive environment so that it inspires others to do better through positivity, not fear. Use positive words like "We got this! It'll be hard but it's temporary! We'll be stronger and faster tomorrow."

- **Don't save your energy for the final sprint.** Conditioning practice for us always inevitably ended in a few final sprints where a certain time had to be met or the first people done were finished. Coaches will notice if you're conserving your energy for the last sprints and will know you didn't put your ALL into the ones beforehand. Give it your all on *every single sprint* you're told to do. Coach will know who was saving all their energy and dogging it on the earlier reps.

Chapter Four

THE TEAM

Team Bonding (*verb*): Doing on- and off-the-field activities with teammates to strengthen team morale and chemistry; spending an excessive amount of hours (in addition to soccer hours) with your teammates while overindulging on snacks, binging Netflix, and whining about how sore you are from soccer.

Let us set the scene for you...

A pile of jerseys, all splayed out on the floor, number side up, with 20-something players eagerly standing around the pile like the scene from *The Hunger Games* when all the competitors are waiting for the signal to run and grab their weapons. You're anxiously eyeing your favorite number, No. 11, and checking your peripheral vision to see if any of your teammates have their eyes locked on the same jersey as you. Coach calls the seniors first to grab their jerseys as you silently say a few prayers to the gods that the No. 11 jersey will remain untaken. Time passes slowly. You're sweating and growing impatient as the pile of jerseys is dwindling down and only the absurdly high numbers like 34 and 91 are left. Finally, coach calls your grade year to go and choose your jerseys. You force a very calm and unfazed look on your face

as you speed-walk as fast as your legs will allow you in the direction of your preferred jersey because you don't want to look too aggressive or desperate. You beeline it toward the No. 11 you're so attached to and as you bend down to grab your jersey (totally disregarding what size it is), your teammate's arm appears and snatches the jersey right before you can grab it. You angrily look up at her, ready to battle over a piece of clothing, but quickly realize you have to change your death stare to a smile because it would be a little savage for you to fight each other over a uniform, right? So, you politely smile, and grab the next jersey to your right. Ahh, good old No. 27. This will have to do.

Isn't that exactly what it feels like whenever it's time to choose your jerseys? The reason we bring up this hilarious (and sometimes scary) scenario is that getting along and learning team dynamics is a big part of being on a team. Let's get real...you are going to spend a *lot* of your time with your teammates (sometimes even more time than you get to spend with your family and friends). There will always be a mix of personalities; people who are like you and unlike you, very competitive and very relaxed personalities, goofy personalities and serious personalities, all mixed together. It's important to be able to let your common goal of being a successful team unite you all, regardless of your differences. And this starts with being able to not sweat the small stuff and choose the higher road, always. No. 27 is the new No. 11, right!?

CREDIT: Sophie Nicholson

Team Chemistry Dos

- **Aim to be on a team that has a good sense of camaraderie on and off the field.** Team chemistry is imperative to the success of a team. From your visit to campus, you should be able to get a feel for team chemistry in the locker room, at pregame, postgame, team dinner events, etc. If the girls make you feel comfortable, that's a good sign. If the girls make you feel uncomfortable because they're being such weirdos together, that's an even *better* sign.

- **Include everyone.** If you plan on going to the movies and it happens to be with seven out of nine girls on your team in your grade, throw the invitation out to the other two girls. They may want to come, or they may not, but you'll never know just how much that invitation could mean to someone on the team (especially when everyone's new). It doesn't feel good to ever feel left out of something. We've all had

soccergrlprobs ✓ ...

When I want to wear something new, I borrow my friends T-shirts #SGP @SoccerGrlProbs that happen, and feeling left out or isolated sucks! Extend the invite to everyone. You may end up having a great time with a teammate you weren't originally close with.

- **Be someone's reason to get better.** We all have someone we admire and look up to who may not even know they are our source of inspiration! The way we carry ourselves, the example we set, the way we talk to others, our work ethic on the field, and the way we can lead from the bench are all ways we can be a source of inspiration to someone without even knowing it. You can be a source of inspiration for a teammate at any given moment. Someone around you looks up to you for something, whether you know it or not. So keep being that person for your team who makes you want to be better. Keep being the person you want to look up to when you are down. You never know who's watching, and you never know who you're inspiring.

Team Chemistry Don'ts

- **Don't be negative, unsupportive, or selfish.** You are a part of something bigger than yourself; be there for your teammates mentally, physically, and emotionally. When a team has good rapport and chemistry, that dynamic can sometimes allow your team to beat an opponent that may be more talented than you on paper. You want to be a team that plays with heart and loves each other—we like to call it our "secret weapon."

- **Don't talk trash about teammates, even if they are asking for it.** Talking behind teammates' and coaches' backs *will* get back to them (and it ain't gonna be pretty). You don't want to be that poison who spreads and infects a team's mentality and chemistry. If you want to vent about someone, write in a journal or call your parents. Don't say it during a team workout or in the locker room. It will only bring bad karma and truthfully, it's a sign of immaturity. You're better than that, girlfriend. If there is an issue that continues to bother you about a teammate or coach, talk to them about it in a non-confrontational way. Address the situation in a way that can bring a positive change and better understanding on each side. There are two sides to every story or situation. You aren't always right or wrong; there is a middle ground in every situation!

Respect Dos

- **Respect the coaches' and captains' guidelines to help the team run smoothly.** You'll receive respect in return. Every team needs structure and a collective understanding of how things go so that everyone is on the same page.

- **Be mature when speaking to other teammates, captains, or coaches.** Communication is key! That doesn't mean you're supposed to have zero say; college soccer is normally a democracy, and there's a time and place for speaking your mind, but not at the expense of your leaders. (This brings us back to picking the right school for you; some coaches prefer a dictatorship!) There are appropriate ways of making your feelings heard...so tread lightly.

- **Compete!** Healthy competition motivates each and every person on a team. If someone is starting over you, you better step up the level of competition at practice. By keeping a high level of healthy competition within a team, your coach can be sure he's got his best 11 out there for that game. The second-string team should be right on their backs, ready to take their starting spot. Purposely injuring the person you are battling for a starting position would be the opposite of healthly competition.

Respect Don'ts

- **Don't be catty.** Come on; we don't want any "on Wednesdays, we wear pink" situations. You will of course have teammates you are closer with, but never leave out teammates from get-togethers, lunch in the cafeteria, or movie nights. The way you behave toward underclassmen will dictate how they, in turn, treat younger classes in the future. It will negatively affect team chemistry if certain people are consistently left out of the loop. You can have your alone time with friends, but why not have a team get-together every now and then to boost team morale? Don't know where to start or how to organize a team get-together? Order food. If you order food, they will come.

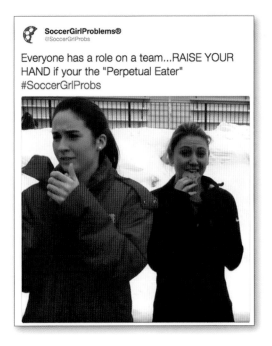

SoccerGirlProblems®
@SoccerGrlProbs

Everyone has a role on a team...RAISE YOUR HAND if your the "Perpetual Eater" #SoccerGrlProbs

- **Don't be offended when being instructed to do something better.** Some athletes don't take constructive criticism well. Don't let your feelings take over. Take this information in, digest it, and do your best to improve this aspect of your game. Coachability is an underrated trait in college soccer. In the rare case that a teammate will badger you with harsh criticism, pull them to the side and explain how you feel in a calm and collected manner. If that doesn't work, then take it up with the coach as the mediator. Chances are the teammate will change their way of communicating, apologize, and you'll both move forward. As our teammates always used to say, "Onward and Upward!*" (*in weird English accents).

Roles Dos

- **Know what role you play on your current team.** Be honest with yourself and aware of where you thrive and include that when pitching yourself to college coaches. However, don't forget to be open-minded about taking on new roles. If coach needs you to play in a different position to suit what the team needs, give it a shot!

  - **Tip:** Make a strengths and weaknesses chart for yourself. Be confident in what you know you can bring to a team. But also be aware of where you can you improve and what you need to work on.

- **Ask what your role on the field might be should you attend a certain school.** On the field, your position or role is super important, especially when making transitions to other positions. For example: if you're an attacking center-mid, you could probably make the transition to winger pretty easily if needed. The transition may take a little more work if you thrive as a defensive midfielder. Pay attention to the role of each position in college, because you never know where you will end up.

- **If you don't know your unique role on a team, just ask a coach.** After just one season of playing he'll know what your superpowers are and why they're important.

- **Off the field, your role is just as significant.** This could include but is not limited to:

  - **Team Mom:** She's always looking out for the younger girls and baking delicious treats postgame.

  - **The Clown:** Her jokes are necessary during water breaks and make the miserable moments not so miserable.

  - **The Hair Braider:** Without her hands, we would all play with our hair down.

  - **The Professor:** She's a wizard of knowledge and tutors everyone on long bus rides, whether it's a class she has taken or not.

  - **The Suck Up:** She comes in handy when no one else read the scouting report and Coach is about to have a nervous breakdown. She proudly sweeps in with the correct answer before you have a chance to get it wrong.

  - **The Troublemaker:** Self-explanatory. Don't be this person.

  - **The Cheerleader:** Your relentless optimism and positive cheers are what gets the team through awful fitness sessions.

- **Respecting your teammates and their roles is important whether you're a senior, junior, sophomore, freshman, or even the team manager.** Regardless of what your role is, make sure that you're a positive force and a respectful role model. Listen to us! Each part of a machine has a specific job. The machine can't thrive if one part refuses to work!

CREDIT: Abby Lydey

Roles Don'ts

- **Don't treat the freshmen like crap.** Yes, it is well known that freshmen will probably hold a lot of the responsibility to take care of the menial jobs that nobody wants to do. These may include but are not limited to: pumping up the balls before practice, picking up all the cones, washing the team laundry if you're in college (gross, but unfortunately there will be a time when you have to ask some teammates to claim their lost and abandoned thongs), grabbing the pinnies for away games, cleaning up the balls, etc. All these tedious jobs suck, but on most teams those are the jobs you're responsible for as a freshman, and as you get older, the will be passed on to each incoming class. It's tradition and a rite of passage! Everyone will get a taste of what it feels like to be a freshman, so as you age, be gentle to the incoming freshmen. You were there once, too. It is important to note the difference between underclassmen responsibilities and being flat-out hazed. If something doesn't feel right, it's probably not right. Talk to an adult.

- **Don't talk back to the seniors.** This is their final season—possibly ever—and they're probably panicking that their time is coming to an end. This might make them just a wee bit on edge or make them psychotically intense during games or practices. Know that it's only because they want to make the most of their remaining time.

- **Don't change the music the Locker Room DJ puts on.** Every team has one. The title of Locker Room DJ is bestowed upon a chosen individual who is in charge of the music during all locker room sessions before practices or games. This individual often guards the music like it's their newborn baby and only plays their favorite songs, regardless of whether the rest of the team enjoys it. All you can do is sit back, try to drown out the sound of Post Malone's "Wow" for the 3,496th time, and pray next week a new Locker Room DJ will take over. Perhaps you can suggest a team Spotify playlist so you can make sure to sneak in your favorite jams. Check out our Spotify gameday playlist!

- **Don't assume that "more scholarship money" equals "more important role."** Whether you received a full-ride, a partial scholarship, no scholarship, or you are a transfer athlete or a walk-on, don't let this dictate the impact you can make on your team. If you do happen to have a scholarship, refrain from bragging and stay humble.

- **Don't consider those on the bench any less valuable than those in the starting lineup.** Competition within the team can only make everyone better. Respect those who aren't starting just as much as those who are, because it takes a whole team to win a game. You're only as strong as your weakest link! Besides, being on the bench means you can sneak snacks in mid-game without anyone knowing…

We know team dynamics can be crazy! It's like having 20-something siblings together all the time. There are bound to be arguments and disagreements, but it's important to remember that the success of your team greatly depends upon how you treat one another. If you all have each other's backs in real life, you will surely have each other's backs on the field. When we are all genuinely rooting for each other's success, the energy is contagious—and those are the teams that can't be stopped! This kind of success starts with the little things. If you see someone being interrupted in a conversation, acknowledge them; don't let them be pushed to the side. If you see someone lagging behind, walk beside them. If someone is being ignored, take the step to include them. Always remind people of their worth. That small gesture can mean a lot.

A little bit of kindness goes a long way. Most of us know what it feels like to be left out or ignored or to feel unimportant. It feels *awful*. A small act of kindness, five seconds of your time, a "you'll get it next time" to a teammate, an invitation to hang out, an acknowledgement of someone's hard work…any of these could make a world of difference to someone. When we treat others the way we wish to be treated, the positivity is contagious. You can greatly impact team chemistry by simply being kind and inclusive of everyone. A team who truly has each other's backs will go further than talent would take them alone.

Chapter Five

POSITIVE SELF-IMAGE

Positive Self-Image (*noun*): Being able to look in the mirror and know that underneath all those scrapes, bruises, baggy sweats, and crazily knotted ponytail stands a confident, determined, and powerful woman.

It's a tough world out there in Instagramland, with endless images of tiny-waisted, big-bootied Instamodels being thrown in your face all day, every day. We find we're constantly comparing ourselves to this so-called "ideal" image. Today more than ever, so many people get lost in trying to be just like somebody else. It's okay to admire others' looks, but if we are constantly striving for all the things we're not, we'll find ourselves empty, unhappy, and endlessly chasing down this idea of "perfection." What's on the surface is just that, surface; it's what's on the inside that counts so much more!

We always jokingly say this, but it couldn't be more true: **We are not like your average females!** Our bodies are machines that allow us to do incredibly awesome things like run our butts off for 90 minutes up and down a field, survive the beep

CREDIT: Keara Russell

test, resist getting knocked down on a 50–50 ball, or have stronger legs than our guy friends. We are athletes and we come in all shapes and sizes. Our performance, strength, confidence, and overall badass-ness is far more important than what we look like on the outside.

It's true; sometimes being a dedicated athlete comes with some not-so-ideal accessories. You may end up going to the Homecoming dance with turf burn on your knees. The first day of school may find you rocking a pair of crutches and a big boot. A summer day at the beach might reveal some wild T-shirt and shin guard tan lines. But at the end of the day, these are the battle scars that mark our strength, hard work, and dedication to something we love. Being flawless is so overrated! Embrace the imperfections that are part of your journey. At the end of the day, the goal is to be able to look in the mirror and love who you are, *inside and out*. Now, we know it's easier said than done, but it all starts with being proud of yourself!

Positive Self-Image Dos

- **Wear what makes you feel best.** All that we ask is that you always try your best to be 100 percent yourself, 100 percent of the time. Don't let anyone make you feel like you have to dress one way or look like someone else or follow some silly trend that you don't even like. Focus more on the inside, less on the outside. Ya dig?

- **Embrace your body!** You are a full-time athlete. Your body and mind are what got you to where you are now—own that. Elite athleticism comes with a multitude of bodily changes. New muscles, bad tan lines, and turf burns and bruises are everywhere. What we're getting at is that this sport can change your body in a million different ways. But all those ways just go to show just how much work you've put in, so be proud of your body, no matter how "imperfect" you may think it is.

- **In fact, embrace your *body type*.** Most clothing items on the shelves are made based on a model's body type. For example, if a shirt does not fit your broad shoulders the way you want it to, that's okay—don't wear things if you don't feel good in them. You don't have to fit into any mold, girlfriend. Wear what works best for *you* and most importantly, what you feel *comfortable* in.

- **In terms of makeup and external appearance, it is 100 percent acceptable to be all-natural.** Who has time to put on a face of makeup after practice? Not us. In fact, you can (ahem, *should*) wear sweatpants to class. We all did it and loved every comfortable, mushy second of it. You are a beautiful person. Don't think you need makeup to prove it, or the added stress of trying to look photo-ready going to each and every class.

- **If you love dressing up, rock it, girl!** If you have time on a Friday and you're going out to dinner with friends, get as dressed up as you want if it will make you feel good. Are we noticing the pattern of self-value yet? Because that's what it's all about: *you* and how *you* feel. Plus, you'll blow the minds of everyone who's used to seeing you in practice gear, smelling like a used sneaker.

  - **Warning:** Wearing jeans and your hair down randomly one day may result in your professor marking you as absent if she can't recognize you for the life of her.

- **As Beyoncé once said, "If you got it, flaunt it."** You have muscles and you are beautiful. Strong is the new sexy. Rock those turf burns and multicolored bruises. Show off those shin dents with pride. It builds character and it tells a story...no lie, it's a conversation starter. Besides, other athletes will immediately connect with you because you're so chill and real. Did we mention that you are chill and real? Because you are. You laugh at yourself, you make mistakes, and you rock grey-on-grey jumpsuits in a way that NARPs (Non-Athletic Regular People) can only dream of doing. You're a confident, magnetic, authentic Ladyballer who everyone wants to talk to. Don't shy away from being an athlete—own it!

- **If you want to make positive changes in your body, that's great!** Just make sure you are doing it for you. Set goals that are healthy and align with your athlete lifestyle.

- **If you are starting to feel negative self-image is consuming your daily thoughts, talk to someone.** Seek out a friend, parent, teammate, or guidance counselor or look into ways to help motivate yourself to be more positive about your body image. This could be anything from reading self-help books to joining a Facebook group to listening to podcasts.

✓ *Check it Out*

Listen to our podcast, *Sh*t Soccer Girls Say*, on iTunes, SoundCloud, or Spotify!

Positive Self-Image Don'ts

- **Don't feel peer-pressured to wear makeup, tight clothing, or anything that makes you uncomfortable.** Express yourself the way you feel most beautiful. Do it because it's what *you* want to do, not because of what others want you to do or because of what you see in magazines and on television. You don't need glitter or head-to-toe sequins or crop tops to stand out (unless you want them). You've got those hot-as-hell scars and calluses that will have everyone weak in the knees.

- **Don't be ashamed of your muscles.** Shift your mindset to focus on the fact that your legs are healthy and you can sprint and lift and do amazing things. Your legs and arms have literally carried you to where you are. Every goal you've scored or ball you've stolen or save you've made is due to them. You worked for them. You've earned them. Be proud. 'Nuff said.

- **Don't hide your banged-up legs!** We swear, if we see you wearing pants when it's 90 degrees out just because you're trying to cover up your bruises and bad tan lines, we're going to have to have a talk. It's too hot for that nonsense!

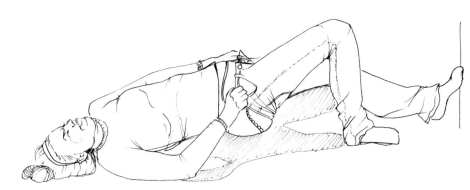

CREDIT: Keara Russell and Hannah Effinger

You are a warrior; embrace your battle wounds and be proud of them!

- **Most importantly, don't compare yourself to others!** As a wise man named Dr. Seuss, our homeboy for years, said, "There is no one alive who is Youer than You!"

We'll leave you with an incredible quote from Alexandra Franzen that we want you to always remember: "You are Gifted. You're a compendium of innate talents, acquired skills, hard-won lessons, and intuitive glimpses. There is no one who can do what you do, in precisely the way that you do it. There is no comparison, and no competition. How miraculous is that?"

Today and every day, let's remember to practice **self-love**. Take a few minutes to yourself right now and think of three things you appreciate and love about yourself. Really think. It doesn't matter how little or unimportant you may feel these things are, because they are what make you special. We all must love ourselves first, before loving anything else. We must keep in mind that we cannot make people like, love, understand, validate, accept, or be nice to us. We can't control them, either. But the good news is, *it doesn't matter!* If you are to do one thing differently from here on out, let it be that you walk toward everything in life being as authentically and unapologetically *you* as possible. Compromising yourself and your beliefs for the approval of others is a quick way to lose yourself. At the end of the day, we don't need validation from classmates or teammates or strangers. We need validation from ourselves when we look in the mirror.

Chapter Six

NUTRITION AND THE IMPORTANCE OF SLEEP

Hangry [*adjective*]: When you're exhausted, bad-tempered, or irritable as a result of hunger.

The only thing worse than a hangry Ladyballer is a *tired* and hangry Ladyballer. Balancing sleep and nutrition among the many other things we have to worry about is a skill even we haven't mastered yet! Come on; how on earth, between classes and homework and studying and eating and practicing and games, are we supposed to be keeping track of our hydration levels and sleep schedules? The key to making significant changes in the right direction is to make *little* adjustments and tricks and habits that you can maintain in the long run! Making a million changes to your lifestyle can often be very hard to maintain over a long period of time. If the changes we make are too extreme right off the bat, we often can't keep up the effort it takes to change everything at once and give up. So try making slight changes and creating brand-new habits from those slight changes. Once those

changes stick and have become part of your regular routine, then you can add in more.

Food is tricky, because everyone's bodies react to everything in different ways and you can drive yourself crazy with all the nutrition info flooding the internet. One simple trick we've found helpful is to keep a food journal. *No*, we do not mean write down every calorie your body consumes and track everything like crazy. We just mean to make note of foods you eat and how they make you *feel*! Maybe we decide to have two slices of pizza (yum!) before practice, but then we quickly learn we're running around feeling sluggish and can't maintain our energy levels. We'd make note that high-fat, greasy, or cheesy foods are not the best choice before a game or practice. Next, we could try a better choice of food before practice and see how that makes us feel, until we find the best choices for our bodies!

When it comes to water and hydration, the opposite is true. Just drink *more!* It's so important for so many reasons, and we all could probably use to have more of it throughout our day. So get yourself a fancy, reusable water bottle and make it your new best friend.

Last but certainly not least, *sleep*. Gosh, we love sleep. So many crucial things happen while we sleep. This is the time our brains regenerate, our bodies recover, our muscles repair, and we recharge for the next day ahead. Now, we may have no control over what time we have to wake up in the morning, but we do have some control over when we go to sleep. Try getting in bed earlier, even if it's just 15 minutes earlier than you're used to. We should be getting around eight hours of sleep at least, and the truth is, most of us are not getting that much. Another great way to get yourself to bed earlier is once you lay down, get off your phone. Some of us can stay up an extra 30 or more minutes mindlessly scrolling through social

soccergrlprobs ✔ ...

♥ ♡ ▽ ⬚

Liked by **mjfayy** and **15,355 others**

soccergrlprobs If you've never taken a nap like this, are you really a soccer player? 😅 ⚽

media. Leave your phone on the charger and let your brain power down and prepare to sleep! This is key to your recovery.

These little food, hydration, and sleep tips can lead to new, healthier habits forming. Overtime these will drastically change your performance for the better!

Nutrition Dos

- **Drink tons of water.** Your hydration levels are key to a multitude of aspects of being an athlete. Proper hydration will keep your core body temperature from rising too high. It'll keep you alert and aware, give you a quick reaction time, and keep your body functioning at high intensity. Not drinking enough water can be disastrous to your body. Temperature and humidity levels can contribute to even further levels of dehydration, and with dehydration comes decreased reaction time, increased risk for fainting, disorientation, heat exhaustion, and even heat stroke (none of which are a joke). *See our nutrition FAQs on page 68 for how much you should be consuming!*

- **Pack a snack for when you're short on time.** You may be apprehensive to try and cram an entire meal down your throat in the 20 minutes you have between class and practice. However, getting something nutritious in your stomach before exerting yourself at practice is imperative. This is where snacks come in. A granola bar or banana or quick PB&J sandwich can be the perfect little boost of energy you need to get through practice. More often than not, you should eat nutrient-dense foods and snacks like peanut butter and an apple, chocolate milk, trail mix, or a grilled chicken wrap.

- **Enjoy team breakfast, pregame lunches, and pasta parties as much as you can.** Not only is Coach paying (we used to call our coach "Dad"...do as we say, not as we do) but, whether you think so or not, you are team bonding!

"I'll run it off later."

CREDIT: Abby Lydey

Our favorite thing to do was to show up and sit down with a teammate that we didn't speak to often. It helps strengthen the bond of the team. You may find that the "shy freshman" ends up being quite the comedian.

- By doing this, Shannon found other teammates who liked music and started an impromptu ukulele band that performed at team pasta parties.

- **Educate yourself on how different foods react with your body.** Some will give you energy, some will make you feel sluggish. Everyone's body is different. See what foods are the best fuel for you!

Nutrition Don'ts

- **Don't get Google-crazy and overwhelmed with all the information on the Internet!** You can drive yourself nuts with thousands of nutrition articles written by lord knows who. Make sure you understand that there are thousands of perspectives on health and nutrition, because what works for one person may not work for another! The key is to experiment with different foods and note what works for you.

- **Don't skip breakfast!** We're not suggesting to gorge yourself at the buffet-style breakfast at IHOP (although that does sound very appealing). Find a food or meal that works for you. Some of us have very sensitive stomachs and there's a fine line between feeling nervous and flat-out nauseated. It's important to find something your stomach can tolerate during workouts and that will keep you properly energized. Remember, calories literally equal energy. Set your alarm an hour early and eat so you have enough time to digest before the session starts if you have to. High-intensity exercise with zero nutritional energy can result in dehydration, fatigue, cramping, lightheadedness, and fainting. For those of you who notice these symptoms, try to incorporate food and water beforehand.

- **Don't eat junk food constantly.** Yes, yes, yes, we strongly support enjoying your snacks every now and then. Our favorites are chocolate, game day waffles, French toast sticks, Swedish Fish...the list goes on forever. Hey, if Michael Phelps can do it, so can we! However, we need to keep in mind the big picture: winning the conference title and the NCAA Championship. Fueling our bodies correctly in order to excel on and off the field is imperative, so keep in mind healthy habits.

- **Don't binge.** It will make you feel sick, keep you from achieving your goals, and lead to a difficult relationship with food. You may feel, after a big win, like celebrating with food is okay, or that, after a bad loss, going to 7-Eleven and buying a ton of snacks will make you feel better, but if you can't keep your portions under control it will end up making you feel exhausted, inflamed, and unmotivated, three things you do not want to feel the next day at practice.

- **Don't under-eat.** You're an athlete! Your body does far more work than the average student sitting at a desk all day. When you Google "How many calories should a female consume in a day?" it's going to throw back a number around 2,000 calories. Don't take this number so seriously; 30 minutes of soccer can burn upward of 300 calories, and that's just playing for fun. One preseason session alone will include warm-ups, high-intensity technical and fitness drills, shooting and passing drills, small-sided and full-field scrimmaging. College soccer players can easily burn more than 1,000 calories per day while training in preseason, and hundreds per day during the season. It is absolutely vital that you replenish what you've lost, and in a healthy manner that will contribute toward repair and growth.

Nutrition FAQs

Q: What are the three macronutrients?

A: You might know macronutrients as "macros." These can seem extremely confusing and scientific at times. Our bodies are complicated! Let us break it down into bite-sized pieces—and remember, you should always talk to your doctor if you have questions about your health.

- **Protein:** Breaks down into amino acids, which are crucial to building and repairing your muscles! We need protein for an array of things like organ repair, recovery, and strength.

- **Fat:** Breaks down into fatty acids, which are absorbed into our lymphatic system! Healthy fats basically tell our body when we are feeling "full" and satiated. Fats are also essential for our hormone health and how well our cells are absorbing nutrients into our body.

- **Carbohydrates:** Break down into blood sugar, which can be either utilized as energy or stored. Carbs are great for future energy use, but if over-consumed, they could turn into fat. If under-consumed, you can experience sluggishness and fatigue!

  - **Complex carbs:** Any carbohydrate that has fiber, like berries or potatoes. Carbs that have fiber tend to be plant-based and are derived from whole foods. We love focusing on these carbs more often than not because fiber is incredible for your gut health and bowel movements.

  - **Simple carbs:** These are refined and processed products or manmade products like candy, white bread, white pasta, and pressed juices.

- **Sugar:** Yes, sugar is a carb! Try to avoid going overboard with sugar because it can leave your blood sugar spiking and crashing. This may leave you feeling exhausted and starving. Hello, vicious cycle of sugar cravings. No bueno for athletes!

High-performance athletes are recommended to have around 30 percent of their calories come from carbs! That is around 150g on average per day, depending on what works for you.

Q: What are your favorite food options that you suggest for female athletes?

A: We absolutely love focusing on whole foods first because we know that is where we find our cleanest sources of protein, healthy fats, and complex carbs! It makes us feel so good on and off the field. Here are our favorites:

- **Protein:** Chicken, ground turkey, grass-fed beef, wild-caught salmon, shrimp, seafood, spirulina, beef jerky, quinoa, pea protein, brown rice protein, protein powder, lentils, and beans.
  - For those Ladyballers who eat a plant-based diet, you can get your daily amounts of proteins from veggies, nuts, and grains.
- **Healthy Fats:** Avocado, nuts and seeds, eggs (with yolk), organic full-fat dairy, extra virgin olive oil, avocado oil, coconut oil, and kefir.
- **Carbs:** We like to focus on veggies first and foremost, like broccoli, spinach, kale, arugula, asparagus, and more. Other complex carbs we enjoy are brown rice pasta, rolled oats, sweet potatoes, and fruit, such as berries.

Q: How much water should I drink?

A: First of all, always carry a portable water bottle with you! It helps to keep refilling the bottle throughout the day so you are never dehydrated. When it comes to specific amounts, here are some suggestions:

- **Before play:** Two to three hours before you play, we recommend drinking approximately 16 ounces of water (one water bottle).

- **15 minutes before play:** Drink 8 ounces.

- **During play:** Try and drink 4 ounces of water every 15 to 20 minutes (two to three big gulps).

- **After play:** We recommend drinking 16 to 20 ounces of fluid to replenish water lost during exercise through sweating and respiration.

  - If you are already feeling thirsty, odds are you are already dehydrated, because the thirst response occurs as a result of dehydration. Don't let yourself get to this point! Bottoms up!

  - Water down your sugary sports drinks before and during exercise! Too much sugar can cause an upset stomach. In addition, although the sugar and carbs in sports drinks may be good for fueling you during and after play, watering down the sugar will help lessen the blood sugar spike.

Q: I get confused about what to eat before, after, and during activity. Can you help a Ladyballer out with suggestions?

A: We want to emphasize that every single person is different! What works for us may not work for you. You can try our suggestions, but then adjust depending on what you and your body needs. Consult a nutritionist if you need more advice.

- **Pre-play:** Try and reach for meals that contain a lot of energy! Look for high carbs, a moderate amount of both protein and healthy fats to help give you energy on the field or in the weight room. Without the adequate supply of carbs, your performance can be limited!

    - **Example:** Our favorite go-to is a peanut butter and homemade strawberry jelly sammy!

- **Post-play:** At the moment the final whistle blows, it's time to shift your focus to recovery. This meal should contain a mix of high protein, moderate carbs, and fat. The purpose of this meal is to help replenish your body, or "refill the tank," to help you recover before your next fitness session, practice, or game.

    - **Example:** Our favorite go-to is a choco-banana split protein shake.

- **Before or after strenuous activity:** Look for a meal high in glycemic carbs and sugar preferably from fruit or a whole foods source. Timing this meal within the proper window before or after strenuous activity is best! That way, these high-energy calories can be put to work. Try not to overindulge!

    - **Example:** Our favorite go-to is fresh mango, pineapple, or grapes, a chopped apple with cinnamon, or coconut water!

Q: I never know what a portion size looks like unless I have a measuring cup handy...which is never! Do you have any tips on portion control?

A: Yes! We actually love referring to our hand when it comes to portion control! Here are some tricks you can use when you're not home with access to your measuring spoons or cups.

- **1 cup:** The size of your fist when you squeeze your hand tightly.

  - **Example:** This is awesome for serving sizes of almond milk for your protein shake or cup of coffee!

- **1 ounce:** The size of your thumb (like you're trying to hail a taxi).

  - **Example:** Great for portion sizes of healthy fats, like almonds!

- **1 to 2 ounces:** Make a cup with your hand.

  - **Example:** Again, great for portion sizes of nuts and seeds!

- **3 ounces:** The palm of your hand.

  - **Example:** This is a great way to tell how much protein you should have! For example, cut a piece of chicken breast and measure it in front of the palm of your hand!

- **1 tablespoon:** Thumb knuckle to fingernail.

  - **Example:** This is awesome to measure fats such as nut butters, grass-fed butter, or cream cheese!

- **1 teaspoon:** Index fingerprint.

  - **Example:** This is just a little bit smaller than the tablespoon.

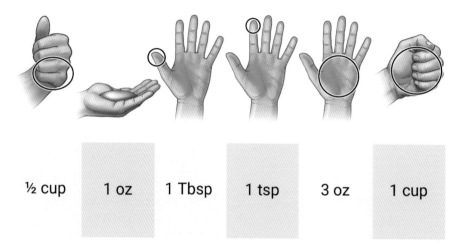

| ½ cup | 1 oz | 1 Tbsp | 1 tsp | 3 oz | 1 cup |

Ladyballers, you may be thinking, *Whoa, this is information overload!* That's because it certainly is a lot to bite into! As we mentioned above, please experiment with yourself. The moral of the story is to find the nutrition that helps you perform the best and on and off the field. Experiment! Add foods in, take foods out! Honestly, you know your body better than anyone, and if you just listen to what you need, when you need it, and how much...you'll be just fine! Yes, that even means in real life, like in the classroom.

If it helps you, here are three signs that your diet is working well for you and your performance:

- **You have tons of energy!** You wake up feeling refreshed and have sustainable energy throughout the day.

- **You're rarely "hangry."** You are consistently eating well-balanced meals often enough for you to never reach the feeling of dying hunger. Your blood sugar is stable!

- **You're recovering after games, practice, and fitness relatively quickly!** If you find that you are not recovering as fast as usual, focus on foods that will help you build and repair so you can be stronger and faster!

You got this, honey boo boo.

Sleep Dos

- **Find the amount of hours that works best for you every single day.** The sweet spot for most is between 6 to 8 hours. This is crucial to your recovery!

- **Act like a child and make a bedtime!** We're not kidding here. When you make a set bedtime, your body begins to

CREDIT: Sophie Nicholson

recognize a routine. Naturally, your sleeping hormones (like melatonin) will raise at the appropriate hours so that you get sleepy during that time! It keeps your circadian rhythm (natural and internal process that regulates your sleep-wake cycle) in check, and you'll be feeling *so* good on a daily basis. Consistency is key here.

Sleep Don'ts

- **Don't skimp on sleep.** We hate the saying "I'll sleep when I'm dead," because truly, if you're not getting enough sleep, you are actually aging yourself! Big time! When you are sleeping, you are recovering. You'll feel so much better at practice or fitness the next morning if you get your z's.

- **Don't stay on your phone until an hour before bedtime.** Smartphones are incredible technology, but they can impact us negatively at times, too. We find ourselves scrolling aimlessly on Instagram and draining our brainpower. Before you know it, an hour will go by and what have you accomplished!? The blue light from phones can actually disturb your sleep cycle long after you've turned off your phone, too. A good tip is to plug your phone in to charge far from your bed so that you can't reach it.

Chapter Seven

INJURIES AND HOW TO DEAL

Injury (*noun*): What every athlete tries to avoid. From something as minor as an infected blister to the full-blown trifecta of torn ACL, MCL, and meniscus. Long story short, injuries *suck*.

Recovery (*noun*): Doing everything in your power to come back stronger and return to the game you love.

Injuries. *Ugh*. Cue the horror music and shrill screams. If you're an athlete, you probably rate "injuries" as No. 1 on the *please don't let this happen to me* list. Injuries flat-out suck. There's no pretty way to say it. They hurt, they're frustrating, they take a *lot* of patience, and worst of all, they keep you from playing the game you love. For a lot of us, an injury of some sort will be inevitable...unless you're #blessed. From ACL tears to back injuries to sprained ankles to concussions to broken hands; the list goes on and on. Between the three of us, we've had more injuries than you could even imagine from soccer. Maybe you've already experienced a significant injury. (And no, we're not talking about a toenail falling off. Although, *ouch!*) OR maybe you haven't yet. Either way, there are some

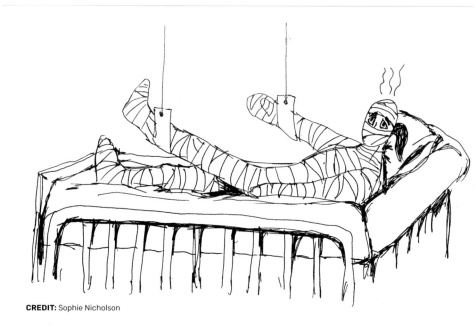

CREDIT: Sophie Nicholson

things to keep in mind and some ways to approach it that will help make it a little less painful for you.

They say that being an athlete is a full-time job. Try being an *injured* athlete. In addition to the 40-plus hours of schoolwork, travel, training, video analysis, conditioning, and games to attend every week, you also spend countless hours in the training room with your athletic trainer/psychologist/ best friend/mom. The thing about a physical injury to our bodies is that it often turns into one that ends up mentally affecting us as well. Our confidence gets all sorts of messed up, we get frustrated and defeated, and we often feel left out of a lot while we patiently rest and rehab. So take it from us, you're not alone if you're feeling this way. We've got some tips for you to help you stay sane through it all.

Injuries and How to Deal Dos

- **Try your best to stay healthy.** Your coach wants his players to be in the best shape possible during the season. If you get injured (#SoccerGrlProbs), make sure that you're in the training room as often as possible. Trainers are there to help you heal. You're lucky enough to have an entire staff of trainers looking after your health...utilize them!

- **Wear your shin guards.** College soccer is a different animal. You'll immediately notice that the level of aggressiveness increases from high school to college! Also keep in mind, you might be 18 playing against a 23-year-old!

- **For the savory love of pizza: stretch!** It's tedious and takes time and is about as boring as being in goal when

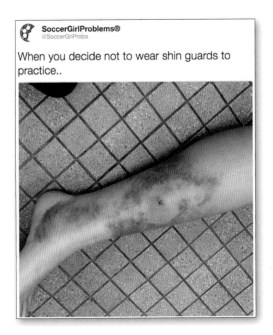

your team is up 10–0, but it's crucial to your success as an athlete and can be one of the biggest factors in preventing an injury in the first place. Warm up properly, cool down properly—taking the little time to do this before and after practices, games, and training will be crucial to keeping your body at its best.

- **Listen to your body.** If you have a nagging pain or feeling that won't seem to go away, don't pretend it doesn't exist and fight through it. Sometimes these lingering, minor issues can turn into full-blown injuries if ignored. Go to the trainer or see a specialist; you would rather find out the problem as soon as possible so you can find a solution!

- **Be the first to the training room before and after practice and games.** There is nothing worse than waiting in line to get your ankle taped behind 15 of your teammates. (Coach does *not* love when you run onto the field mid-warm-ups.) Actually, we lied. There is something worse than that: waiting in line for the ice bath. This could take a good 30 to 40 minutes if you are on the end of the line and if you have class, you're stuck skipping the ice bath and hurting the rest of the day. A wise soccer gal once said, "Early bird gets the best tape job and first ice bath."

- **Rolled up towels under your armpits if you're on crutches are a *lifesaver*.** The pain that crutches causes to your armpits from relying on them so much is sometimes worse than the actual injury itself. Just kidding...but not really. So grab the duct tape and some washcloths your mom won't kill you for taking, and tape those babies to the top of your crutches. This will save you a lot of armpit pain.

- **Assess and discover your imbalances!** When our bodies are imbalanced, or we rely on one side more than the other, it sets the perfect scene for an injury! Go and see your trainer or strength and conditioning coach and have them assess you. Take a look at your squat. Are you squatting in a healthy manner or is it uncovering some weaknesses? Is your right leg as strong as your left leg? Do you have good balance and stability on both limbs? Is your core (abs, back, upper trunk) strong? All of these factors and more can play a role in how prone to injury you are. And there are corrective exercises that can help fix imbalances and weaknesses!

- **Brace yourself for *everyone* to ask you about your injury.** The questions are endless, and if we had a nickel for every time someone cracked a *Bambi*, *Forrest Gump*, or *Transformers* bionic knee joke, we would be living on a private island somewhere lost in the tropics.

- **Be kind to yourself.** Give yourself the time. Understand that there will be good days and bad days and that it is okay to get frustrated. It is okay to be upset. Be patient with yourself.

PHOTO CREDIT: Daphne Youree

- **Always, always, always get back up.** After your said allotted recovery time, get back up. Make moves to come back stronger than ever. Find that group of friends, family, teammates, or coaches who build you up, and surround yourself with them every single day.

- **Stay involved.** This might be the most important rule. Go to practices and games. Cheer your teammates on. Be a presence for your team. Don't feel like you can't contribute to the effort just because you can't be the one making the plays. Your time will come.

- **Take baby steps back into it.** Make sure you are paying attention to your body—if you start to notice old injury symptoms or new injury symptoms creeping in, be honest with yourself *and* your physical therapist! It may mean slowing down your progress. Fast progress is not worth it if it's going to result in a big step back! As one of our preschool teachers used to say, "smarter, not harder." (You're so wise, Miss McAllaster.)

- **Meet your new best friends: foam roller and ice bath.** They will make your body feel terrible and amazing simultaneously. It's a love-hate relationship, but you're in it for the long haul. For those of you who have never had the pleasure of being introduced to either of these, here's the lowdown. A foam roller looks like a giant rolling pin that you essentially use to massage your muscles. Now "massage" is a word that sounds relaxing and enjoyable, but let us assure you that your experience will be neither. The idea is to roll various areas of your body over the foam roller to break up adhesions, scar tissue, and knotted muscle fibers with the goal of speeding up the recovery process and increasing bloodflow. Ice baths are used to help soreness and healing, as well. You put the desired area of your body (sometimes your entire lower body if needed) into the ice bath. It is believed that the cold temperatures constrict the blood vessels of that area temporarily, helping to flush waste products and reduce swelling and tissue breakdown as the blood flows back to those areas.

- Some tips we've gathered over the years regarding these two torture devices: when it comes to foam rolling, the only way you're getting through it is to suck it up. (Talk about good advice, eh?) Your best bet is to distract yourself; talk with someone while you do it, listen to music, eat a snack…*anything* to take your mind off the agony you're experiencing at the moment.

- As for the ice bath…well, that's another story. *Do not* try and ease your way into it. Dipping your big toe in slowly will only convince the rest of your body that there is *no way in hell* you're getting in that thing. Also, the little booties they provide for you at the trainer's office? Wear those; they're lifesavers.

- **(Kindly) force a teammate to come in with you.** Even if they're just standing there, a BFF nearby and talking to you is a key distraction to keeping your mind off the cold water. Keep telling yourself that this insane tub-of-hypothermia death is worth it, because you'll come out of it feeling like a new woman!

Injuries and How to Deal Don'ts

- **Don't think you can't make a difference just because you're injured.** It means a great deal when an injured teammate still shows up to all the practices and lifts instead of blowing them off. You can still be a source of inspiration, motivation, and positive energy, even when you're sidelined.

- **Don't stop learning.** This rule—like all the others, if you haven't caught on yet—should be followed for life. You are either getting better or you are getting worse. There is no staying the same. If you can't improve your game on the field, improve it in other areas. Get extra fit. Lift more weights. Eat healthier. Be a student of the game. Study what people do with the ball and think about how to play smarter. You will get your touches on the ball when the time is right. In the meantime, keep getting better.

- **Don't fake an injury to get out of conditioning, fitness tests, or traveling to an away game.** We know weekends spent traveling to far-away games in the middle of nowhere aren't always your most fun option, but being an NCAA student-athlete is a privilege. You made the commitment, so don't lose the respect of your coaches or teammates on a whim. Even if the lacrosse team's party is that weekend, realize there are bigger things going on in your life. No one wants to hear that you tore an ankle ligament to miss an away game and then see you wearing high heels at a party on Instagram. That's a one-way ticket to getting singled out.

- **Don't overdo it when your injury needs rest.** We know this is insanely hard. You have been training at such a level that your brain thinks going for a light run instead of a death sprint is considered "rest," but it is in fact not. Those extra fitness sessions on top of training on top of practice can lead to dragging out your injury for longer and keeping you away from what you love most—*playing!* Plus, you are an athlete. Your ability to stay in shape and/or get back to playing like you used to is significantly higher than the average human being. (Thanks muscle memory; you rock.) So just trust us, and rest when needed.

- **Don't lie about an actual injury or illness.** If you're sick or have a lingering injury (big or small), don't be a hero. You're not helping the team if you're struggling through an injury and bringing down the level of play. If you have a sprained ankle, the trainer needs to know about it. It's so important to catch a problem before it gets worse and sidelines you (pun intended) for an extended period of time.

- **Don't fall asleep with ice on your body.**

  - Fun (and beyond embarrassing) fact about Alanna: in preseason she had a hip injury, and during preseason *all* you want is to feel your best and be able to perform. So she was icing like a madwoman, praying to numb the pain to be able to play. In between sessions during a three-a-day, all your time is spent eating and sleeping. She decided it would be a great way to kill two birds with one stone by icing *and* napping at the same time. (It sounded like a great idea at the time.) Fast-forward to after a nice three-hour coma with a bag of ice on her hip, Alanna woke up with *frostbite and ice burn.* Her trainer actually laughed at her when she told him, because what idiot leaves an ice bag on for three hours? Anyways, we hope you've learned something from this. Ice for 20 minutes at a time, please.

- **Do not make comparisons to yourself pre-injury.** You're setting yourself up to be frustrated, and it's only making your comeback harder. Track the progress you make post-injury and take every victory (those extra drills, faster workouts) and celebrate it. Eventually, you'll return to "old you" workouts and times, but you aren't the "old you," you are *even better!*

CREDIT: Abby Lydey

Chapter Eight

BALANCING SOCCER AND SCHOOL

Athlete Multitasking (*verb*): The act of trying to win a conference championship while putting in more than 40 hours a week of games, practice, technical, fitness sessions, and simultaneously completing your homework, writing 10-page papers, and studying for your tests; all of which reaffirms your loyal commitment to your one true love: soccer.

If you're a high school athlete, you have a laundry list of priorities: excel in school; put in maximum effort at practice, games, tournaments, and showcases; take care of your body; do research; and prepare for college and more. We understand that there are hundreds of sacrifices that you'll make throughout your career. However, sacrificing a nap to study for a midterm, or sacrificing a party to hydrate and rest before a big game, or even sacrificing *prom* because you're away at a college showcase (true story) is all worth it in the long run. You may not believe us now, but trust us: going to your top-choice school because you dedicated the time to get

there is *priceless*. Playing for a team that you've never dreamt you'd be able to play for is an unmatchable feeling. Give up a little to earn a lot. Oh, and have we mentioned that you're completely and totally not alone? Any college teammate, or even opponent, will have made sacrifices of their own, too.

Especially as you play at a higher level (varsity, collegiate, or pro), it can be extremely challenging to fit in time for others, let alone any time for yourself! It's not easy to balance soccer, school, and a social life when you are committing multiple hours a day to the sport that you love. We know sometimes all we can think about is soccer, but when we take a step back, our No. 1 priority (outside of family) is our schoolwork. Our grades will determine the colleges we can go to and the degrees we get for our eventual careers, so it is important we don't let school go on the back burner while all our efforts go toward our sport. As athletes we should pride ourselves on excellence in all aspects of life, so crushing it in both soccer *and* school is an awesome quality to have as a student-athlete. Now, we know; it's easier said than done, and that's why we've compiled some tips for you to be your best in both areas. Not to mention, if you are staying on top of your schoolwork and are staying prepared, this will drastically reduce your stress and allow you to focus on your sport and be present when you are at practice.

Staying Organized Dos

- **Prioritize!** What is important to you in season, postseason, or in the offseason? It's crucial to understand and see what is most important to you when trying to schedule your time.

  - **Tip:** Make a list of your top three to five current priorities. If it's down on paper, you know it's real.

- **Make a game plan!** We know how overwhelming it can be when you have big goals or important things to focus on, but you don't know what direction to move in! We find it so helpful when you write down the steps (big and small) that you need to take to achieve those goals or bring attention to those priorities. When you organize your thoughts in this manner, you might feel less stressed. Woo-hoo!

- **Sticky notes and reminders in your phone are a game changer!** We know you are a master multitasker, but don't put that pressure on yourself to commit everything to memory with no help. Instead of trying to keep all the things you need to do as a running list in your head, write down your reminder to print out a paper or study for a test and let the notes be your motivator.

Staying Organized Don'ts

- **Don't fall behind on schoolwork!** Seriously; make it a priority! There is a risk that if your GPA dips too low, you won't be able to play on the team. It has happened to some of our teammates in the past! If you need extra help, communicate that to your teachers and your coach. They might give you opportunities to make up some work to improve your grade!

IN SEASON

CREDIT: Sophie Nicholson

- **Don't skip your study hall hours or extra help (especially if you are a freshman).** Extra help could mean staying after school and seeing a teacher to get some clarity on something you didn't fully understand in class. Study hall hours, for those of you who aren't in college yet, are mandatory hours given to you by the athletic department that are essentially forced homework time. (It sounds fun, we know.) With so much time devoted to your sport in high school (and even more so in college), it's easy to be clueless as to how to balance everything. That's why once upon a time, someone invented study hall hours for athletes. The amount of study hall hours depends on the division of your program. And yes, they're mandatory. If you have study hall hours, you *must* fulfill the requirement for the week. Otherwise, your coach will find out and make you go to your away opponent's library to finish homework while your team is warming up for the big game. (It happened to Shannon.)

Time Management Dos

- **Set alarms on your phone to go off a little bit before they need to!** Hear us out. We feel like setting alarms are great, but giving yourself that extra time is even *greater*. We personally find this to be very helpful when it comes to waking up and getting ready for the day. You'll have an extra couple of minutes to collect yourself, double check your backpack, and eat something before you head out and crush the day. You'll want to avoid the extra stress on your heart before you head to conditioning.

- **You've heard this before...but time management is a major key!** It can be intimidating fitting in studying and writing papers between practice, technical, fitness sessions, extra fitness, talks with coach, and team social or volunteering events. We'll never forget one of us crying our eyes out in the locker room after practice from feeling overwhelmed from school and our soccer schedule. We were viewing our week as a hot mess rather than tackling each thing one at a time in an organized manner.

- **Schedule everything.** Literally, block off times for when and where you have things going on—even your nap or "free" time! Schedule *everything* into your calendar on your phone or in your room. You might feel more in control of your hectic days, weeks, or months. Try it!

- **Strategically schedule classes (if your school allows you to make your own class schedule).** This is extremely crucial if you have the opportunity to pick your class times or off periods if you are in high school. Luckily for in-season athletes, more often than not you get to pick first for classes before the rest of your classmates (#AthletePerks). This is key so that you can schedule classes around your practice and game schedules. Make sure you pick realistic times so that you're not overwhelmed rushing from one class to another and then straight to practice.

  - **Tip:** Ask older teammates about certain professors, because there will be times when you need to miss a class because of an away game or mandatory soccer event. Also, communicate with your professor early on and bring a note from the athletic department for when you have scheduled games and have to miss class. You'll be A-OK! Get it? You'll get an A grade!

- **Utilize your travel time!** Chances are, during the season you are on the road more often than you are home. Bring your textbooks and utilize your travel time on buses, trains, and planes to get your studying and homework checked off your *already hectic* checklist. Write your 10-page paper in all of four hours on the way to your away game or the hotel!

Get it done before you play; you'll probably be exhausted after 90 minutes...you can reward yourself with a nap rather than homework assignments!

- **Fit in a social life!** Ladyballer, let's be real. You've lost count of how many proms, Sweet Sixteens, and bat mitzvahs you've missed in your lifetime because "you can't, you have soccer." Sometimes, we're just too tired to even go out and socialize! This is where we can go wrong. Part of having a well-balanced life is to hang out with your friends and family. (More on this in the next chapter.)

Time Management Don'ts

- **Don't waste your time.** You become a master of your life when you learn how to control where your attention goes. Value what you give your energy and time to. There's a really simple way to help determine your priorities and what you give your time to. Try filling in the following sentence: *I (do or don't) make time for _____ because _____ (is or isn't) a priority in my life.* Fill it in, read the sentence back to yourself, and say, "Is this what I believe and how I feel?" Here are some examples:

  - **Example:** *"I don't make time for injury prevention exercises because my health isn't a priority in my life."* Hmm, now that doesn't sound right, does it? My health *is* a priority to me, but my actions are not aligning with it. Maybe it is worth me putting some of my energy toward that.

  - **Example:** *"I do make time for studying because school is a priority in my life."* That sounds about right and is something I believe in, so I will continue to put my effort toward that.

- **Example:** *"I do make time for scrolling through Instagram for an hour before bed because it is a priority in my life over getting a good night's sleep."* Except I'm tired *all* the time. Maybe I will make an adjustment and only scroll for a few minutes, because a good night's sleep and being well-rested *is* a priority to me.

Remember, Ladyballers: *time is a currency that is nonrefundable.* You are the decider of what you get to spend your time and energy on. And the power is in your hands. Make sure you are spending it on things that align with the priorities you have for your life, whatever those priorities may be.

- **Don't start your day sprinting to class or practice as fast as you can on an empty stomach because you woke up late.** Starting your day off on the wrong foot sets the tone for the rest of the day. Feeling rushed and "all over the place" can be a heart-throbbing, stressful way to start your day.

- **That being said, don't be late.** In season, out of season, spring season, summer preseason; it doesn't matter which season...don't be late. Make sure your alarm is always on and loud enough to wake you up. Set that frickin' thing up across the room if it will get you out of bed. You and your alarm clock will be besties. Make sure you wake up in time to be on time, which we should point out, means *geared up and ready to go 15 minutes early*. As our college coach always said, "If you're on time, you're late." It also helps to make your alarm sound is something you enjoy waking up to, such as a pump-up song—anything by our girl, Lizzo. That will help you feel a little less sad and a little more pumped up before a 6:30 AM conditioning session.

- **Don't run on exhausted, burnt out, smelly fumes.** Make sure you are getting enough sleep and recovery after your long days. We like to think of sleep as a dishwasher. You turn it on before you go to bed so that the dishes are clean and ready to be used the next morning. Your brain and body need to rest, recover, and repair so that you are ready to tackle the next day sparkling with energy and a clear mind. You will feel much more stressed and burnt out if you are not taking care of yourself!

CREDIT: Sophie Nicholson

Picking a Major in College Dos

- **Pick a major that aligns with your passion...but more importantly, your soccer schedule (haha, only kidding!).** Shout out to you collegiate #Ladyballers who have to choose your major at some point during school. We know how stressful it can be trying to find a major that works well with your soccer schedule. Usually, nursing students or engineers have a hard time finding the healthy balance between labs, studying, and soccer practices or games! If you haven't gotten to school yet, do some research on the university and its majors!

- **Ask your coach about his policy with students who have more time-consuming majors.** How can you both work together to make sure you can pursue what you want in school as well as be the best athlete you can be for your team?

- **Ask around the team or contact the team captain.** Does the team currently have student-athletes who are pursuing the major you want? How does their schedule work with soccer? Ask for tips and tell them to be honest!

- **Explore your interests.** If something sounds appealing to you but you don't know much about it, try giving that class a shot. You may end up discovering your major!

Picking a Major in College Don'ts

- **Don't go to a school only because you like their soccer team!** Make sure that you are thoroughly researching the majors that they offer and whether they align with your future career goals! We hate to say it but, remember, you won't be playing soccer forever. (Unless you want to!)

- **Don't feel pressured to make up your mind on your major before you are ready.** Often we experience so much pressure to decide our major that we pick something just to say we did. Then, later on we end up changing our minds as we discover our true passions at school, and this often leads to a bunch of wasted money on classes that you didn't end up having to take. Being an "undeclared" major is okay!

SOCIAL LIFE

Social Life (noun): A type of enjoyable, carefree time that NARPs have, but you probably won't because you're too busy saying, "I can't, I have soccer."

Let's face it, our social lives are like the endangered species they talk about in an Australian accent on the National Geographic channel. It's always a rare sighting to see a soccer girl at a social event, because our schedules just don't allow us much time for socializing. Plus, it's just so heavenly to lay in your bed at the end of the day wrapped in various shades of grey sweatpant material. But when it comes down to it, the right balance of socializing can be great for you, allowing you to have some stress-free and unscheduled fun. It's nice to do something for a change that doesn't make you think,

 SoccerGirlProblems®
@SoccerGrlProbs

I can't, I have soccer. #SGP

Okay, practice starts at 5, so I should get there by 4:30 which means I should leave the house by 4:15 so I should probably start getting ready at 3:45. Whether it's socializing, dating, or even social media, there are ways to sprinkle it into your already crazy lifestyle that will help bring more balance to your life!

Be Social Dos

- **Socialize when you can!** Mark off time to go see a movie with a friend, go out for a fancy dinner, binge Netflix, play board games, or go bowling. (Bowling is actually cool. Don't let people tell you otherwise.) There are so many responsible, fun things you can do socially that don't involve making poor decisions.

- **Go out and meet NARPS.** For those of you who don't know what a NARP is; it stands for Non-Athletic Regular Person. We're not quite sure how this term even originated, but it's used among college athletes. Soccer friends are the best friends, there's no denying that. However, keep your mind open when meeting new people at school. Meet people from other sports, people who don't play sports at all, upperclassmen, and underclassmen. Socially, college is a buffet; who says your friends have to be from the same part of the long buffet table? On a similar note, it's okay to surround yourself with or even room (if you're in college) with a non-soccer person. If your entire life is soccer-related, you risk getting burnt out. We highly encourage you to break outside the soccer world a bit. Scary, we know. College campuses especially are overflowing with fun, supportive, and relatable people who you will never meet if you don't spread your wings. Having friends outside of soccer will be a good change of pace. All three of us soccer ladies roomed with girls who played other sports like volleyball and softball and even some non-athletes. Every time we walked into the living room, we relaxed and bonded with other friends who cared about us! We had more in common than you'd think!

- **Make friends in your classes.** We know it can be difficult to form friendships with new people, especially if you are more introverted, but having class in common is a great way to break the ice and start a conversation with new people.

- **If you're new to a team (which we all are at some point in time), start a conversation!** Let people get to know you. We know it's easy to be shy and hide off to the side when you're new, but remember odds are there is at least one person, if not a bunch more people, on your team who you'll end up loving and getting along great with.

CREDIT: Hannah Clayton

Be Social Don'ts

- **Don't let FOMO get to you.** Just because you have a game the next day doesn't mean you need to say "no" to everything. Remember, your social life is *just* as important to your mental health as the physical and emotional side of things. Our best advice to you is to for every invite you say no to, say *yes* the next time. Even if you go to the party or event for 30 minutes, go show your face and get some social time in! If you have time, go grab a coffee with a classmate or join a campus club! Just make sure that it's not playing another sport; your coach will not want you getting hurt.

- **Don't break the "Team Rule."** Every team is different, but chances are your team will have some sort of rule about social life, parties, and drinking during the season. You're still allowed to be social! Just respect team rules and the captains when they set guidelines to keep your team focused and in the best shape possible. You've dedicated so much of your time to being healthy and in shape and tackling your goals, so why bother putting substances into your body that go against all the care you've given it? After all, your goal is to win championships, isn't it? If it's not, then what are you doing there?

- **Don't get in trouble.** This section is pretty self-explanatory. Coach won't be happy. Your team won't be happy. The athletic department won't be happy. And lastly—and maybe the scariest—your parents won't be happy. You are a representation of your team, both on and off the field. Be smart about what you do. Otherwise, your coach will wake your butt up for 6:00 AM fitness and run you sick...#Regrets.

▪ **Flashback:** Two hours of running our massive library hill at 6:00 AM because of a certain teammate. Still burned into our memory. We might even still be sore. Punishments suck, and you'll never forget them.

Dating Dos

- **If you do want to date, that's awesome!** If you don't want to date, that's awesome, too! When dating, find a significant other who fully understands that he or she will be sharing you with your 20-something other teammates and who also deeply appreciates "sweatpants, hair-tied, chillin' with no makeup on."

- **Find someone who will support you.** *Heck yes* they should come to all your home games if they are able to. You work hard, and you deserve someone who wants to be there for you. Bonus: If they are a fellow athlete, they can work the women's soccer games and get some volunteer hours in. It's a win-win.

  ▪ Carly's husband played on the baseball team. He always told her he'd be watching all 90 minutes of her games. She thought it was the sweetest thing, until she found out he was being paid to be there as a ball-boy.

- **Find someone who will listen.** Your sport will be frustrating at times and having someone to talk to who isn't in the middle of it all is key. At the same time, find someone who knows when you're not in the mood to talk about your game and perhaps offers a hug and a trip to Chipotle instead.

- **Find someone who loves you whether you're dressed down or dressed up.** If your significant other has a problem with the "athletic look," and by that we mean sweaty and

crazy hair, baggy sweats, and turf burns everywhere, then he or she may not be right for you.

- **Find someone whose heart is as big as your appetite.** Seriously though, they've gotta love you enough to be able to handle your appetite. We've never eaten in front of a mirror, but we can imagine we ain't too cute at the dinner table.

- **Calf massages.** 'Nuf said.

SoccerGirlProblems®
@SoccerGrlProbs

Female Athlete Tip #147: Find someone whose heart is as big as your appetite.

Seriously though, they've gotta love you enough to be able to sit down across from you while you relentlessly shovel enough food down your face to support a full-grown man.

Dating Don'ts

- **Don't date anyone who makes you choose between them and soccer.** You are a girl with a lot of strengths and priorities. Finding the balance between school and sports and friendships and relationships is hard, but if anyone can master it, you can. You don't need someone making this process a stressful one for you.

- **Don't be with someone who brings you down.** You've got dreams and goals and you work your tush off every day to

CREDIT: Keara Russell

be the best you you can be. Be with someone who pushes you to be better and encourages you to dream big!

- **Don't use dating as a distraction.** Yes, it's nice to hang out with your friends or boyfriend or girlfriend to take your mind off school and soccer if you are stressed. However, they can't be a permanent escape for you. If you are constantly going to your significant other to run away from other things in your life, this may not be healthy for you. Instead, be with someone who can allow you to de-stress, but also keep you motivated and inspired.

- **Don't feel pressured to date at all.** You may be more interested in forming friendships than going on two awkward dates with that jerk Kyle who doesn't even want to order dessert.

School Activities Dos

- **Join groups and clubs around school.** We realize it may sound lame now, but there are so many extracurricular activities you can be involved in that not only help you meet new people and make new friends, but are also great resume builders. Employers want well-rounded women, not *just* Ladyballers. Good at math? Join the Mathletes! Love movies? Join a film club! Love throwing balls at other people? Dodgeball leagues are everywhere.

- **Go watch the other teams' games!** Supporting the other sports at your school is part of being in the big family that your athletic department hopefully is. Not to mention, it's fun to scream your head off about a game that isn't your own every once in a while. Odds are, you've got friends on other teams at your school so why not go and support them!

- **Find a part-time job.** If you have the time and are looking to make some extra cash for all those Nike leggings you've been dying to wear, find a job that works with your crazy, busy schedule. It may be working the clocks at other athletic games, tutoring, or babysitting. Find something that's flexible and won't crush you with your already busy schedule.

- **Volunteer!** We are all so blessed to be able to go to school and play soccer. Giving back feels good. It makes you feel like you can make a positive impact on someone else's life. We volunteered with a kids' soccer clinic on Saturdays and had so much fun (even though it was really early to get up on our off days, LOL).

  - Shannon went to New Orleans with Habitat for Humanity on Spring Break and built a house. It was a great way to meet new NARP friends and help people in need.

School Activities Don'ts

- **Don't play in a contact intramural league while you're in-season.** Your coach will *not* be happy. That sprained-ankle-from-falling-down-the-stairs lie won't fly when someone from the men's basketball team tells your coach he saw you fall while horsing around playing pick-up. It'll earn you a spot on the bench along with some marathon punishment runs to follow. And while we're on the subject, don't lie! The truth always comes out and it's just better to own up to your mistakes in the beginning rather than let a lie spiral out of control. At the end of the day, a good portion of your off-field time should be dedicated to schoolwork and taking care of yourself.

- **Don't overbook yourself.** You may be eager to try an array of new things, but just remember, your schedule is already crazy. You want whatever additional activities you sign up for to be ones that add an aspect of positivity of your day, not more stress.

Social Media Dos

- **Keep your social media clean.** Everyone is looking at you, *especially* if you are a college athlete. Deans, professors, the athletic department, and students; they're all Googling you. Student-athletes are a representation of the university or college they attend. Everything you put out on the Cloud, Facebook, Snapchat, Twitter, Instagram, TikTok, and other social media channels will find a way to be permanent. Snapchats can be saved as screenshots, and we haven't even brought up text messages. Long story short—trust the people with whom you associate and communicate and be smart about it! We've had teammates lose scholarships and be suspended because of poor choices of social media photos. Learn from their mistakes.

■ **True story:** A high school friend who was committed to play lacrosse at her top university had her offer taken away by the college after they found pictures of her partying on Instagram! It's crazy to think, but social media now serves as a representation of potential recruits. So when you are applying to school or for a job, keep in mind that whoever is looking at your application can very easily find your social media, too!

CREDIT: Keara Russell

- **Make your social media accounts private.** And on top of that, make sure any picture you post, any picture posted of you, and captions you write are appropriate. Every time you go through your photos ask yourself, "What would Grandma think if she saw this?" That'll help. Unless you've got a really wild grandmother. #Respect

- **And, of course, double check that you're following us on all social media channels to help keep you laughing.** Handle: @SoccerGrlProbs.

Social Media Don'ts

- **Don't talk smack about a teammate, coach, teacher, faculty member, or an opponent on the Internet.** Players all over the country have been suspended for social media jokes gone wrong or bad-mouthing others on social media. Don't write anything when you're emotional. In fact, don't write anything negative at all. Unless it's a funny soccer girl problem; then you're safe.

- **Don't post "sexual" or "skimpy" photos on the Internet.** An easy rule on this: don't post anything you wouldn't want your grandparents or parents to see. Even your Facebook profile picture in your mini-skirt and crop-top will circle around the athletic department and get back to your coach. We're not saying to not be proud of the way you look; you should be! But at the same time, your coaches and school administrators worry about you as they do their children. You are wonderful and fantastic as you are. Just think twice about the public image you put forth into the world.

Chapter Ten

CHAMPION MINDSET

If there was a "most important chapter" that can contribute to your growth as an athlete, human, goal-crusher, and overall badass woman, this one might take the cake. We like to think of our mentality as the little voice inside our heads. The way we speak to ourselves day in and day out will dictate the way we walk through every part of life. Will we speak to ourselves with a positive and encouraging voice, or one that beats us down and doubts us? Will we speak to ourselves in a way that motivates us to reach higher and do more, or will the voice inside our head fill us with thoughts of mediocrity? Will we speak to ourselves with forgiveness when we make a mistake, or will we only hear defeated and negative thoughts? This little voice inside your head determines the mindset that you have going into every single situation; whether that be our schoolwork, our relationships with others, our sports, our dreams, or our aspirations.

Like our bodies, we feel that our minds can be trained, too, with practice, discipline, and understanding. A positive, uplifting, relentless, driven mindset doesn't just happen overnight. However, we can do things like read, meditate, and practice to flip the switch and change our mentality over time.

So what does it take to have a champion mindset? Are you willing to develop yours? Because only *you* have the power to do it. There's a book called *Champion Minded* by Allistair McCaw, and in it, he has an incredible definition of champion mindset. He drops this truth bomb: "You are not born mindset tough. You choose to be. Getting mindset tough means enduring experiences in your life. From those experiences, champion minded athletes and people develop grit. What is grit, you ask? It's the ability to overcome challenges and to endure hardship. It's about handling and overcoming failure, and it's about getting up one more time after being knocked down."

Amen, am I right? Grit is not something everyone has, and it's hard to teach. Some of the most talented athletes lack grit and relentlessness, and this holds them back from reaching their true potential. Grit is cultivating your *why* and your *purpose*, then finding a true, deep sense of *belief* in this vision. And, finally, relentlessly getting after it. So ask yourself, "What is my *why* and how am I going to ensure I will stop at nothing to chase it?" You don't always have to be the most talented player on the field or court. Attributes like *grit* and *heart* can often overpower talent.

The champion mindset is a weapon you can develop that has nothing to do with the body you were born into or your skill level. It is an entirely different aspect of your game that you can conquer. Are you going to be someone who can dig deep when times get tough, or will you throw in the towel? Are you going to say, "Yes, I can" when the world is shouting "No, you can't"? Are you going to wake up and get to work regardless of if you feel good or terrible that day? Are you going to choose to go over the hills instead of take the easy route around them? What kind of mindset do you want to have moving forward? How much failure and adversity can you

PHOTO CREDIT: Daphne Youree

face without backing down and giving up? You and only you get to decide.

Champion Mindset Dos

- **Build positive mental habits.** Just like anything else, the practice of a consistent behavior can turn into a habit, good or bad. So when thinking about your mindset, it is crucial to practice *positive* and tough thinking. This plays a huge role in your performance on and beyond the field. If you are practicing mental toughness, you will have mental toughness more often and it will come to you like second nature!

- **Push your limits.** There is a safe zone during training sessions where you feel good, you can breathe, and you're in control. Then there is the zone where you feel uneasy, uncomfortable, and like you're being pushed to your limits.

Your brain will try to think negative thoughts, your heart will race out of your chest, and you'll start to doubt you can handle the pressure. The latter is the zone where you will grow. It will push you past the limits that you create in your head and make you stronger, faster, and better. Gravitate toward that challenge!

- **Learn the art of losing.** Winning is great, but there is something else you need to be great at. Have you ever known someone who is calm, collected, and has it all together when they're winning, but the second they lose or have an obstacle ahead of them, they completely fall apart? That's because there is an art to losing. Losing can't be something that breaks you. The greatest champions in the world have learned their most valuable lessons during moments of defeat or challenge. Losses have to be something we grow from and overcome and triumph over! True champions know how to get hit and come back harder. So take your losses with grace and be open to the lessons they are trying to teach you. Remember, nobody goes undefeated all the time!

- **Be okay with resting and taking off.** Being mentally tough doesn't mean a "no-days-off-never-sleep-never-rest" mindset. We need to understand that our mentality needs to be strong, yes, but most importantly it needs to be healthy! Taking a mental health day or rest day is crucial to not only your body but your mind. Make sure you are blocking off time to *not think* about your performance or school or soccer or fitness. Read a really good fiction book, listen to a comedy podcast, head to the go-kart place with your friends. You'll be better for it!

- **See failure as an opportunity.** The difference between a strong mentality and a weak one is the way we react to failure. When you mess up during a game, do you blame other people around you? Do you sulk or dwell on what you did wrong or poorly? Or are you the person who holds yourself accountable and sees it as an opportunity to get better and learn from it? The key here is to be a strong player who accepts failure, tries to understand what went wrong, and uses it constructively moving forward.

- **Realize that hard work and dedication go so much further than talent.** We asked Alex Morgan for advice in an interview and she dropped some *wisdom* on us: "One piece of advice to my younger self...I would say that hard work and dedication go so much further than talent. I felt so discouraged when I was younger because the girls around me were such better soccer players than I was. But at the end of the day I knew that I wanted it more. I worked harder to get where I am today and I never really detracted from that vision and that dream that I had." Think about that; *the* Alex Morgan, one of the greatest in the *world*, once felt discouraged when she was your age because there were girls around her more technical and talented than her. Let that work ethic and desire of yours push you further than you ever thought possible!

Champion Mindset Don'ts

- **Don't compare yourself to others.** Ladyballers, every single person on this earth is different. That includes athletes, too! We all have different strengths and weaknesses in all aspects of our lives. Sometimes we forget how amazing we are just the way we are. Some may even say our personal and individual strengths are our "superpowers." Today's world makes it all too easy to compare ourselves to celebrities or people on Instagram or even those around us on a daily basis. However, what some people don't realize is that you are comparing your day one to someone else's day 30, day 60, or even *years* of progress! We just want to remind you to stay focused on yourself and your own personal journey. How can you be mentally tough if you are worried about what others are doing or where they are in their journey?

- **Stop dwelling on failures and mistakes.** We touched on this a little bit above. The key to mental toughness is learning from mistakes and moving forward. After a team loss, we would always say "onward and upward." Let's wake up tomorrow with a fresh new start and get back to work to win the next game.

- **Don't get too comfy in your comfort zone.** The longer we stay within our comfort zone, the more discontented we sometimes become with the way things are. But moving out of our comfort zone is *hard;* it takes effort. It's important to remind ourselves of the three reasons our comfort zone is killing us!

  - **First, you're not growing!** Growth is about progress and movement and doing something you're not used to doing. Step outside of what you're used to. Experiences are meant to be had!

  - **Second, you're missing out on new things!** It's hard to discover what we have a passion for if we aren't giving ourselves a chance to experience it. By constantly staying where we're comfortable, we may never actually open ourselves up to the things in life that we're meant to do.

  - **Third, you're teaching yourself to settle.** You don't want to find yourself 10, 20, 30 years from now wishing you had reached for more when you could have. The bubble of comfort is only great for so long. Never settle!

The more we step out of our comfort zone, the less we will resist the tasks that face us in our future. And let's face it; we are always going to find ourselves face to face with tasks we avoid doing (for example, the pile of dirty soccer laundry we haven't washed in a week.) The more we step out of our comfort zone, the less fear we will have of something new. And most importantly, the more we step out of our comfort zone, the more we will build confidence to go after our goals without so many things holding us back. If you're not moving forward, you're standing still. So take a risk, try something new, and discover your passions!

- **Stop playing the blame game.** Don't be that player who is always blaming others for her mistakes during the game. "She should have passed the ball two seconds sooner!" "It's because Coach is playing me at a position I rarely play!" "I didn't play well because the grass sucked and my shoes are so tight I can barely run!" This kind of negativity can not only be draining, but it's also like you're trying to convince yourself of a lie to make yourself feel better. Literally *no one* in this situation is getting better by playing the blame game. So cut the crap; be stronger and tougher.

A huge part of being the best you that you can be is having goals. We all know this. But it has to go deeper than that! What's the point in having goals if you don't believe you can actually achieve them? The reason most people never reach their goals is that they don't define them or ever seriously consider them believable or achievable. Dreams and goals are only as good as your ability to believe in yourself. A huge part of committing to goals is *actually* believing that they are possible for you. A 50 percent commitment to your dreams

will get you nowhere, fast. Have the confidence to follow your heart—it will make all the difference.

We read once that there are three simple rules in life:

1. If you do not go after what you want, you'll never have it.

2. If you do not ask, the answer will always be no.

3. If you do not step forward, you will always be in the same place.

Goal-Setting Dos

- **Invest in a goals notebook or journal!** Writing down your goals and envisioning your future makes you much more likely to achieve your goals.

- **Get specific.** When you're thinking about your goals, you want to be extremely specific and dialed-in on what exactly you want to accomplish. For example, "I want to run a six-minute mile" is a lot more specific than saying "I want to run faster." Write it down!

- **Set goals that are measurable.** Again, you need to get specific here! Quantifiable goals are extremely crucial because hey, how the heck will you know if you've achieved your goal if it was too vaguely described? For example, a good measurable goal is to run one mile every Monday and write down your times. Keep a running list of the data to see if your mile time has improved in four weeks!

- **Dream big, but also think about attainability.** We want you to reach *as high as the stars!* Yes, you are allowed to set your ultimate huge goal in life, but we want to remind you to set attainable smaller goals, as well. We need to find a healthy balance between goals that are too unrealistic and goals that are not challenging enough. For example, your ultimate goal is to start on the U.S. Women's National team by age 21. However, smaller attainable goals could be like making your state ODP team or making the roster at Regional Camp or going to ID camps for the national team. Those smaller goals are more attainable and great steps toward your ultimate dream!

Check it Out

Need a goals journal? We've got you! You can order our Daily Greatness Journal on our website (www.soccergrlprobs.com).

- **Set relevant goals.** Relevant goals are a major key. Does your goal support your personal mission and beliefs? Does it align with what you are "all about?" Does your goal make sense for the time? For example, if you are a soccer player in the middle of your season, you wouldn't be setting a goal to run a marathon in that same season, would you? Nah, girlfriend! Think about what time you are in, how you are feeling, and what your priorities are, and go from there.

- **Think timely.** Let's talk about time, shall we? Having an extremely specific time or date will help increase the chances of you getting it done. Think of it as a milestone that you must hit! We love scheduling this goal in our calendar or downloading a countdown app! It's a great way to hold yourself accountable every morning when you see how many days you have left!

- **Tell your goals to an accountability partner.** This could be a friend, family member, or teammate! You set yourself up for success when you tell another person about your goals. Not only are they your cheerleaders and biggest supporters, but you will want to make them proud by showing up and getting what you have to get *done!* You're one step closer to your goals by cultivating a supportive environment!

Goal-Setting Don'ts

- **Don't compare your individual goals with others'.** This is a big one! When talking about personal development, your goals and your dreams are *yours*, not theirs. We need to stop worrying about others and turn inward to focus on ourselves at times. When we do that, we pour all of our energy into improving!

- **Don't compare your progress to others'.** When we find ourselves comparing our Chapter 4 to someone else's Chapter 20, we feel nothing but stuck and discouraged. We find ourselves thinking, *My classmate already knows where she's going to college and I have no clue*, or *My sibling was already on the A-team at my age*, or *That girl is friends with everyone and I only talk to a few people*...the list goes on. What's important to remember is that we are all on *our own journey* through life. Everyone will have different starting points and speed bumps at different points along the way. You're not being fair to yourself when you score yourself against others without looking at the bigger picture. If we get too consumed worrying about where everyone else is, that's energy wasted that we *could* be spending on ourselves to keep moving forward. Allow yourself time to reach your goals and take each speedbump as it comes. *You may not be exactly where you want to be, but that doesn't mean you're not on your way.*

- **Stop trying to get small wins by aiming low. You'll never improve!** You have to find that healthy balance between unrealistic and way too easy. For example, you wouldn't set a goal to go to practice, because you're already going to practice. A daily task isn't a goal! Ask yourself, *How can I make this more beneficial to my success?* A better example would be to go to practice 20 minutes early to get 100 juggles in a row. Now that's more challenging, attainable, and will help you improve your technical skills!

Staying Motivated and Positive Dos

- **Open your eyes in the morning and start your day thinking about one thing you're grateful for, no matter how big or small.** Let that be the first thing to enter your mind in the morning. A beautiful day begins with a beautiful mindset. When you wake up, take a second to think about what a privilege it is to simply be alive and healthy. Now, it's true; everyone is fighting their own battles of all different sorts. However, when you really stop and think about the little things we take for granted every day and just how lucky we are to have a roof over our heads, food to eat, schools to attend, teams to play the game we love with...it's impossible not to be grateful for all that we have.

- **Clap for yourself.** We know this sounds funny, but seriously, be your biggest fan! The thing about hard work is that it often goes unnoticed until you can do something great with it. But a lack of recognition shouldn't be a reason to stop. It's true; no one sees the person who puts in extra hours at the gym late at night, or the girl who's up late studying while everyone else is asleep, or the last one left on the field once everyone has already left practice. Only you truly know how hard you're working. And you should be *damn* proud of that work. Be your biggest fan. Encourage yourself and motivate yourself to keep pushing to the next level. You don't need others' recognition that you're doing a great job because *you already know*. Just keep at it. Consistency is key.

- **Take your failures and turn them into your fire.** How you view your failures determines where you go next. Your thoughts matter. Instead of saying to yourself, "I can't do this," try, "I can do difficult things." Instead of, "I'm a failure," try, "I'm learning." Instead of, "Why is this happening?" try, "What is this teaching me?" From every struggle, failure, hardship, and mistake comes a lesson learned, confidence gained from overcoming, and a new perspective. If you always ask yourself, "What can I learn from this?" you'll transform your mind from negative to positive. There is something to be gained from everything, even the hard times. Always remember that and just keep going.

- **Choose your influences wisely.** Our favorite Sunday self-care tip is to unfollow every account on social media that makes you feel like you need to be someone else. We often find ourselves following celebrities or influencers who make life look flawless. But as we all know, life is plenty full of imperfect moments! Social media only shows a small sliver of one's life, but we tend to view it as a representation of someone's life as a whole. It can cause us to start reaching and longing for an image of perfection that doesn't necessarily even exist, which can leave us with the feeling like we're always falling short of something. Remember, *we are most influenced by the people we spend most of our time with*. So as you scroll through social media in your downtime, think of who you're letting take up your time. If there's an account or a person who makes you wish you were different for unimportant reasons, *you* have the control over who you see. Hit that unfollow button, girl! Follow people who empower you, or bring a smile to your face, or spark your creativity, or make you want to dream bigger, or be a better human, or remind you how lucky you are to have great people in your life, or accounts that simply post pictures of adorable puppies. We all have things we want for ourselves in our life, but it shouldn't start with wishing you were someone else. Being *you* is the best part of it all.

Staying Motivated and Positive Don'ts

- **Don't lose patience just because you're not seeing progress.** Give yourself time to develop new habits! On average, it can take weeks to develop a habit. (Weeks?! Ahh, so that's why we can't form good new habits. We give up *way* before then!) Think about it. If you've been trying to make a positive change to your life, like adding a mile run to your daily routine, or extra study time to your schedule, or eating a healthier, more balanced diet, and it just feels like work *every single day*, it's because you just need more time for it to become a habit! A lot of the time we get impatient or don't feel a change in ourselves right away, so we call it quits after a week. Don't let yourself give up before you give your body a chance to actually form a *good new habit!* It *is* possible. Waking up earlier, or eating your veggies, or doing extra strength training will over time become something your body is so used to doing, it won't feel like such a job anymore! Never underestimate the power of a new good habit!

- **Don't let yesterday take up too much of today.** Did you
  have a bad game yesterday? Maybe you let a goal in or
  missed a wide-open net? Or maybe you made a big mistake
  in practice this past week, or embarrassed yourself in front
  of a stranger, or bombed a test in school. We all have days
  like that, and they *suck*. But the only thing that makes them
  suck more is to let the negative feelings from that day carry
  over into the next...and the next...and the next. Sometimes
  we hold onto our mistakes because we CARE that much
  and we want our coaches and teammates to know how
  seriously we take this game. Mistakes happen. *It's okay.*
  Give yourself a break. By letting your mistakes negatively
  influence future events, you're allowing them to do more
  damage than they should. Sometimes the best thing we
  can do for ourselves is shake it off, take a deep breath, pick
  our heads back up, and keep going. Remember, we are not
  defined by our mistakes—only by how we respond to them.
  Take your mistakes, place them under your feet, and use
  them as stepping stones to rise above them!

- **Don't get so stuck looking at the bigger picture.** We
  know, we're always hearing "look at the bigger picture,"
  but sometimes, looking at the daunting large goal that we
  haven't achieved yet can make us feel like failures. And
  if we only allow ourselves to be happy when we hit big
  life goals, then we're missing the point. The vast majority
  of your life consists of small everyday wins, not huge
  milestone achievements. If we take a look at all the smaller
  parts that make up that big picture goal we have, there
  is so much to be celebrated. These mini milestones and
  daily achievements can fuel your happiness and a feeling
  of fulfillment. It's all about our mindset and how we look at
  things. Start by becoming more aware—more aware of the
  small changes, the little obstacles you've overcome, the
  negativity you've risen above. Did you run even just five

seconds faster on your timed mile? Did you get to bed an hour earlier because you knew your body needed it? Did you remove yourself from a negative situation because it was hurting more than helping? Did you have a constructive conversation with Coach? Did you make a slight adjustment toward healthier nutrition? Did you handle getting beat on the field in a more productive way? These are all things to be *celebrated*. Sure there is no title or trophy to show for these kinds of things, but these are the puzzle pieces that get you closer to your goals! Allow yourself to feel a sense of pride and accomplishment and happiness for these things, no matter how little they may be. You're on your way to something *big*, and *happiness* isn't only meant to be felt at the very end. It's meant to be felt along the entire journey!

Chapter Eleven

MENTAL HEALTH AND MANAGING STRESS

Not enough athletes talk about their internal struggles and the physical pressures they put on themselves day in and day out. It's time to talk about it. Mental health takes priority over *everything.* Your mental health is more important than the test, the interview, the lunch date, the meeting, the family dinner, the soccer game, the recital, and the practice.

I know what you're thinking. *But SGP, all of those things are not optional, they are things I can't miss and have to do.* But the truth of the matter is, when our mental health starts to get out of our control, all of the above can't be done to the best of our ability and absolutely will not be as fulfilling as they're meant to be. Monday through Friday can be *exhausting.* You're trying to balance school, work, training, family, friends, and *so* much more. By the weekend you can feel like you're running on empty. You've probably put your mental health on the back burner all week *without even realizing it.* This chapter is about dropping what you're doing right now, pressing the pause button for a few minutes, and devoting some time to your mental health. It's okay to put other things on hold temporarily. When you get in a more positive headspace and healthier mindset, all the other pieces of your life will become more enjoyable, make more sense, and *add* to your joy (instead of building up stress).

We hope you'll walk away from this chapter with a better ability to recognize when you're stressed, a greater appreciation for the need to take time for yourself, and some tools to help you relieve stress that you can integrate into your regular week. We promise, it will make all the difference!

As always, we're right here with you...

Just because you're expected to be strong for your sport doesn't mean you have to be strong *all the time*. We are here to tell you you don't have to go it alone and there are healthy ways to manage your stress! Athletes (*also known as superheroes*) are *incredibly strong* human beings. But that doesn't mean we aren't allowed to have our weak moments.

We are constantly held to high standards and expected to be at our best at all times. We are expected to be the strongest in the weight room, the fastest during fitness, to show mental strength after we lose a ball, all while getting straight As, eating a healthy diet, and finding time to spend with friends and family.

We get so used to hiding our weak moments for our sport that we don't allow ourselves to have any weak moments *outside* of our sport. We are supposed to constantly be at our *best* with our heads held high and our emotions pushed to the side because nothing can stand in our way...we are athletes.

You're not alone. No matter how tough, happy, or composed we may look on the outside, we are *all* dealing with stress and emotions underneath that hard exterior. A lot of us have a terrible habit of not confronting our emotions and suffering in silence and more often than not, this leads to things like

anxiety and depression. (*Important note: You may be a Ladyballer who has experienced the above scenario, and that is okay.*)

You can manage your anxiety, your thoughts, and your emotions in a healthy and well-balanced way. You can use certain strategies that work best for you to help heal and guide yourself through any problem that you face now or in the future. And as always, if you need the help of a professional to accompany you through your journey, that is what they are there for! Through our individual experiences, we found that there are some natural strategies that you can implement into your lifestyle and daily routines to help relieve stress. *We challenge you to take a look at our strategies below. What is one thing you can work on today that will help you deal with your soccer girl problems?*

Mental Health Dos

- **Surround yourself with supportive people.** Whether you realize it or not, the people you hang around are very influential to how you feel! If you are hanging around positive friends who support you, you will improve your overall well-being. They will strengthen your relationships and give you that security of always having a shoulder to lean on!

- **Talk to a professional or ask for help.** We are telling you right now, Ladyballer, don't feel self-conscious if you need to speak with a psychologist or mental health counselor! There are hundreds of thousands of people in this world who work with professionals to ease their anxiety and depression and to learn stress-management techniques. (Even professional athetes do!) If you are ever feeling alone or just need an unbiased third party to speak to, please reach out to your local trained professionals at your school or in your town and seek the help you are looking for!

- **Work on your mental toughness (see: Chapter 10).** Please go back to Chapter 10 to see all of the incredible tips and tricks we have on this!

- **Volunteer and give back.** We know what you're probably thinking: *SGP, we don't* have time *to take a nap in between classes, let alone volunteer!* Hear us out. Giving back and volunteering with younger soccer teams or others in the community can give you a sense of joy. You're donating your precious time to help others, and it can truly boost your mental health. The satisfaction of doing something for others is invaluable.

- **Spice things up!** Your daily routine can get stale sometimes, leaving some of us bored, unstimulated, going through the motions on autopilot. Mix things up in your daily life to keep your brain on its toes! For example, take a different walking route to class, try a new workout class, brush your teeth with your nondominant hand. Just switch things up!

- **Spend quality time with friends, family, teammates, or classmates.** It is so easy for us to stay inside to nap and Netflix after practice or games. However, don't entirely exclude yourself from socializing because of soccer! Dedicate a couple of hours a week spending quality time and laughing with friends and family. It's incredible for your mental health!

- **Schedule in technology-free hours.** Speaking of quality time with others, get off your phone when doing so! Work on being present and living in the moment, and worry less about Instagram likes on your recent posts.

- **Purge your social media!** We're not saying delete everyone off your Instagram list, but we highly suggest clicking the "unfollow" button on those accounts that make you think *negatively or critically* about yourself. Purge the accounts that don't serve you! You'll feel like you've just done spring cleaning..ahhhh, refreshed and revitalized.

Mental Health Don'ts

- **Don't be so hard on yourself.** It is so easy to get down on yourself when you mess up or are too hard on yourself after making a mistake. This mindset will *not* serve you! As mentioned in Chapter 10, being mentally tough takes practice. Work on turning your negative thoughts into positive ones. Instead of asking "Why did this happen to me?" ask yourself, "What can I learn from this?"

  - Shannon remembers that during college recruiting she would constantly think negative thoughts about how she was playing when a college coach came to watch her, and that only made her play worse! When she started thinking more positively while playing that was when she would shine most in front of recruiters!

- **You can spend time alone, but do not exile yourself from social gatherings and groups.** As we mentioned before, it's so easy to host a pity party for yourself, stocking up on snacks and locking yourself in your room until you've re-watched every season of *The Office*. However, exiling yourself for long periods of time indoors can be depressing. Get outside and go hang out with friends every once in a while!

- **Don't feel like you need to be like everyone else.** You'll never influence the world trying to be like it. Anyone who

makes you feel like you need to be more like *them* in order to be accepted is not worth your time or energy. Let's be honest; we're all *weird!* Embrace that weirdness, love the things that make you different, celebrate what's unique about you, and proudly be your own person. Because it's much more fun to be loved for who you actually are instead of liked for who you aren't, right? Plus, living like your true, authentic self will lead to much more positive mental health!

- **Don't turn your social media notifications on!**
  This should be the rule moving forward for everyone. Turn all your social media notifications *off (except for SoccerGrlProbs' new posts, podcasts, and YouTube videos… just kidding!).* There are so many great things happening in front of your eyes every day, and notifications on our phone going off all of the time pull us away from being present.

Investing in Self-Care Dos

- **Clean up your diet.** We're talking about shopping smart and investing in cleaner groceries! Your diet and what you're feeding your gut is directly correlated with your emotions and feelings every day. Did you know that studies estimate 90 percent of your serotonin is produced in your digestive tract? That's right! A big part of your happiness depends on what you are putting in your belly! When you think about it, when you are eating foods that don't make you feel good, your brain, hormones, and emotions are not going to "feel good," either! The key here is to be mindful of what you are consuming and put the focus on your gut health. Happy gut equals happy brain equals happy player. Here are some specific suggestions.

  - Focus on eating whole foods first. Make sure your plate consists of quality protein, healthy fats, complex carbs, greens, and fiber.

  - Add in fermented foods like kimchi, miso, yogurt (prebiotics and probiotics).

  - If you don't like any of the above foods you can try a daily probiotic (at least 50 billion CFUS) *The key is to find a probiotic that will survive your stomach acid!

- **Drink water.** When you're drinking enough water, you are protecting your brain from the effects of dehydration *(which is highly likely with high-performance athletes such as yourself)*. Make sure you are always refilling your reusable water bottle throughout the day. You'll feel *so* much better and you'll tackle your day clear-minded, more energized, and focused!

- **Good hygiene.** This might have not even been a thought in your head, but we think good hygiene is extremely important for mental health. Think about it. When you're in your pajamas all day, with unbrushed teeth or hair, and unshowered...how do you feel? Not so good, right? Make sure you are taking care of your daily hygiene before and after practice and games. Your confidence will skyrocket and you'll feel mentally and physically great in your body.

- **Morning notes/journaling.** Writing down how you're feeling is therapy in itself. Get your thoughts out on paper so that you can make sense of them. Read them over. Acknowledge them. Then let it *be*. Don't let all of that get stuck in your head. You already have too many things to think about!

- **Read self-help books.** Invest in a really good self-improvement book that sparks your interest or speaks to you! Those books are so inspirational. You might come across a line and say, "Dang, I needed that right now!"

- **Make yourself a priority.** Whether it's putting yourself first with your time or energy, do it. As athletes, it's easy to forget to take care of ourselves when we are lacking sleep, scrambling to get to class after practice, and eating fried foods and take-out constantly on away trips. Just a friendly reminder to invest in yourself because it pays you back tenfold on the field, in the classroom, and on your journey in life.

Check it Out   Check out our list of empowering and inspiring book recommendations on Amazon (www.amazon.com/shop/soccergrlprobs)!

139

Investing in Self-Care Don'ts

- **Don't bash others to feel better about yourself.**
Ladyballer, you need to learn to love yourself for who
you are. When you bash others, it just stems from your
unhappiness with yourself. Usually, people smack talk
because they subconsciously think that they will feel better
(which truly never works). Self-care is self-love. Work on it!

- **Don't do things that don't serve you and your morals.** We
love this tip because it's something we wish we did more in
high school and college. Say no to going to events or hang
outs with people who are not supportive or impacting you
positively! For example, for the college-aged Ladyballers,
don't get bullied into going to a bar and drinking when you
know that goes against the goals you have for yourself right
now! There are other people, such as other athletes or your
teammates, you can surround yourself with who don't do
activities that revolve around alcohol. Or, do go to the bar to
be social, but just drink water!

PHOTO CREDIT: Daphne Youree

- **Don't spend hundreds of dollars on quick fixes or performance supplements!** Please do not fall for the "detox," "weight loss," or "performance enhancer" marketing you see on teas, drinks, protein powders, and sports supplements that aren't reputable! First, you don't need to spend hundreds of dollars on quick-fix supplements (that's where you go back and focus on cleaning up your diet). However, there are ways you can complement your life and supplement with products that may help you feel good on and off the field. If that's the case, make sure you are *always* investing in trusted and scientifically backed products. Ask your athletic department for safe and NCAA-approved athletic products.

Managing Stress Naturally Dos

- **Sleep!** We know this may sound childish, but it's actually crucial to have a bed time. As humans, our bodies and our hormones *crave* routine! If we start to make a habit of getting in bed at a certain time and winding down, our bodies will naturally cue the output of our sleep hormone, melatonin. When our bodies are producing melatonin at the appropriate time at night, we have a more restful REM sleep. This is the time of your sleep cycle where your body recovers and restores mental function (which processes your emotions). So for the sake of your hormonal balance, emotions, and mental health the next day, don't skip on sleep!

- **Meditation.** Researchers are finding that meditation is a game-changer in improving your mental health! We're living in a world jam-packed with stimulation that can drive us and our thoughts bananas! We are all in overdrive, stressing about one thing, anxious about another—thinking about all of that soccer, school, and social life stress! Our suggestion to you is to download apps like Headspace or Shine and invest in a couple of minutes of meditation a day. Your body and brain will thank you for it, and you may even grow to love doing it.

- **Breathing.** Do you ever feel like, *Wow, I forgot to breathe for a second*? You're not alone! It happens to us, especially when we're feeling stressed and thinking about a million things at once. When you're not breathing deeply, your body tends to think you're stressed or in danger. Compare this to when a rabbit is being chased by a coyote. The animal is in fight-or-flight mode...also known as survival mode! Our bodies think the same when we are not breathing diaphragmatically. So do yourself a favor, and put your phone down. Take 10 deep breaths at the count of 3-4-4 (breathe in three seconds, hold for four seconds, breathe out slow for four seconds). Repeat this 10 times and see how good you feel!

- **Legs up!** You're probably laughing right now thinking about our YouTube video when we put our legs up after games to get rid of the lactic acid! However, we're actually teaching you a way to de-stress and turn on your parasympathetic nervous system (your rest and digest mode) to tell your body that you are safe and A-OKAY! When you lift your legs above your heart, gravity moves the blood flow toward your heart. This helps calm your nerves and helps you de-stress. Try it out!

- **Walk in nature!** If you live near a park, river, or nature walk, go for a leisurely stroll from time to time. Spending time in nature can decrease your stress and it's a great way to start your day on a fresh start or unwind after a day of playing!

  - **Bonus:** Feel the leaves of the trees or grass at your feet with your hands. Think about how it feels to physically touch nature. It helps you become *so* present in the moment.

- **Listen to pump-up music and dance it off!** Last but not least, music is *powerful* and has a total mind-body connection. Thinking in extremes, a good song can bring you happiness and energy while a

Follow us on Spotify for more feel-good and pump-up songs!

sad or depressing song can bring you to a dark place. Let's focus on *happy, upbeat, or calming music* for times that you are not feeling so great. Music can not only drown out your racing thoughts, but it can change the state of your brain chemicals, bumping up the serotonin levels and give you positive energy. Kick off your shoes, start dancing, and shake it off! Here are some of our favorite upbeat songs that can instantly change our mood:

- ▣ "Good As Hell" by Lizzo

- ▣ "Going Bad" (feat. Drake) by Meek Mill

- ▣ "Lose Yourself" by Eminem

- ▣ "Raising Hell" by Kesha

- ▣ "Water Me" by Lizzo

soccergrlprobs ✓   •••

Having a teammate you can vent to about every detail of your life & constantly whine about how sore you are without feeling like ur being annoying/boring is one of the best gifts in life.
10/10 would recommend.

Managing Stress Naturally Don'ts

- **Don't overdo it on the sugary drinks and food.** Everyone hates this tip, because we all tend to have a craving for coffee and candy bars when we are eager to find more energy! However, we must understand that these stimulants can speed up your heart rate, thoughts, and feelings and make you feel even more overwhelmed. In addition, caffeine stays in your system for a while so it can really affect your sleep (which, as we just learned, is super important for stress management). For example, if you have a full cup of coffee at 10:00 AM, you still have half the amount of caffeine in your system at 4:00 PM! And if you have two cups of coffee...well, you get the picture!

- **Don't rely on pharmaceuticals to cure your problems.** Some of us are prescribed medication to help improve our mental health. That's completely fine! Just please know that you should see the medication as a complement to your daily routine. What other ways can you naturally treat the root cause of your anxiety, depression, or negative thoughts? Can you work on your sleep, diet, movement, social life, and more? See the tips in this chapter for ideas!

- **Don't stay inside all day!** Get off that couch! We've touched on this before, but staying inside, getting zero natural sunlight, can actually lead to depressive thoughts and feelings! Open those shades, make your dang bed, and get outside!

Why do we feel like it's so wrong or unacceptable to not feel like ourselves, when this is a totally *normal* part of being human?! It's okay to be going through a rough patch. Believe it or not, if you take a look around you, odds are there are a bunch of people going through similar things. You need to know you are never alone in your difficult times and that a better day can be right around the corner. You just have to keep on going. **Keep waking up,** even if you don't want to face the day. **Keep doing the work,** even if it feels pointless or hopeless (we promise you, it's not). **Keep the things that matter to you close,** whether that's a friendly face that makes you smile or a pet you can cuddle up with. **Celebrate the small victories,** even if that's just finishing a simple homework assignment or going for a walk. The things that bring you happiness, **do more of those things.** Don't be afraid to ask for help. And lastly, never, *not even for one second*, doubt that you are strong.

Let's make a pact: we won't bury our stress if you won't. Deal? You'd be amazed at what hitting the pause button can do for you! Zach Galifianakis has an awesome quote that we try and embrace every day: "Destroy the idea that you have to be constantly working or grinding in order to be successful. Embrace the concept that rest, recovery, reflection are essential parts of the progress toward a successful and happy life."

We try and make these three R-words part of the end of every week: **Rest. Recovery. Reflection.**

If you're feeling worn down or overworked or overtrained or like you're running on empty, it's okay to hit the pause button. If the things you are doing every day aren't bringing you *joy*, let yourself breathe, take a break, and recover. Sometimes a little reflection and a fresh perspective can allow you to enjoy the things you used to love. Remember, all the things you do from day to day are supposed to be pieces of the puzzle to your happiness! So don't let them become something you resent because you aren't giving yourself the rest and reflection you need. We all have some sort of dream we are chasing, and we know we won't get there in a day. You have to pace yourself in order to go the distance it takes to achieve your dreams. We all want to be able to go 100 percent all the time, but the truth of the matter is you can only keep that up for so long before crashing. The three best things you can give yourself are a clear and rested mind, a healthy and recovered body, and a happy and hungry heart. So take time for *you*, Ladyballer. Use rest, recovery, and reflection to get in the zone. Use whatever techniques help alleviate your stress and keep you focused. And then get after it!

Notes to Self

- You cannot and will not please everyone. That is a fact of life.
- By taking care of your own needs, you will sometimes disappoint or even anger other people.
- How other people react to your choices is not your responsibility.
- The greatest responsibility you have is to your own well-being and happiness.

Chapter Twelve

COMMUNICATION

Coach Meeting (*noun*): The most nerve-racking moment of your life (we're kidding, but at the moment you really feel like it is). Your palms are sweaty and your anxiety is through the *roof* as you try to rack your brain about what Coach could possibly say to you. You start to list all the things you have done wrong on the field. After you sink into the chair across from Coach, start tearing up, and feel your voice shaking, Coach ends up going through the most honest and awakening assessment of yourself as a player. You freaked out for *nothing!*

Meeting with Coach Dos

- **If you have a question or concern, schedule a meeting with your coach.** This step is *huge!* You're putting yourself in a better position to not only look proactive to Coach because it shows you care but also improve your game with guidance from the person who controls playing time! If you are struggling with something, make an effort to improve it. Ask your coach if they have time before or after practice to help you. They will notice that you are putting in the extra effort and time!

- ▪ You also have the option to swing by the coach's office even if it is unplanned. They love getting to know you better off the field. (Plus, maybe you'll see what they're plotting up there.... Kidding! Kind of...)

- **Be prepared to talk about yourself: Think about how you've been playing, what you think your strengths and weaknesses are, and what areas you think need improvement.** Homework isn't *just* for the classroom.

- **It's okay if you're nervous.** You may get upset and cry, but just remember this meeting isn't to attack you, it's to help you improve! We know what you're thinking: *Why on earth would I cry in a coach's meeting?* Just trust us, it happens sometimes. Carly once stained her white long-sleeved shirt with makeup from crying in a meeting. Work on going in with a calm, positive mindset. If you think your nerves will get the best of you and you won't remember what you wanted to say, bring notes (and take notes)! This is just another way Coach will see how much you care!

CREDIT: Hannah Clayton

- **Follow up with your coach on your progress every few weeks.** Even a quick text or email will suffice! Make sure you ask the right questions and steer the conversation toward how you can continue to improve. They will appreciate your effort and you'll get the inside scoop on what they're looking for.

- **Ask to do more training outside of practice.** Your coach will be more than willing to meet you out on the field. Your coaches care about your personal development just as much as you do! This is their job, and they will go above and beyond to help their players improve. Don't be afraid to ask to do extra work.

Meetings with Coach Don'ts

- **Don't wait until your coach reprimands you to improve.** Make the effort and communicate with him or her!

- **Don't run into your coach's office shouting, "Why am I not playing?!"** It has never resulted in more playing time and shows you are currently sporting the "me" mentality.

- **Don't take coaches' criticism personally.** Try not to be offended by their feedback. Whether you agree or not, respect their opinion and grow from it.

Communicating with Refs, Teammates, and Parents Dos

- **Always treat your teammates with respect.** Whether it's your best friend on the team or the player you are competing with for a starting spot (or both), everyone deserves to be treated decently. If you do not feel you are receiving the same respect, talk with that person off the field about it or speak with your captains or coach about how to best resolve the issue!

- **Appreciate the refs.** Think about this for a second. Have you ever said after a game, "These refs were awesome"? Chances are you probably haven't. Refs have one of the hardest jobs in the world with very little praise. Always be polite and respectful to refs, even if you don't agree with every call they make. After the game say thank you to the ref and shake their hand. They will definitely remember this next time they are reffing a game for your team!

- **Your parents may have advice for you after a game.** Know that they love you and they care about you, but take their advice with a grain of salt (just as you would with anyone giving you advice). We love our soccer parents, and sometimes they know what they are talking about, but sometimes they don't. You will be receiving advice from coaches, parents, and teammates, so view it all collectively.

PHOTO CREDIT: Daphne Youree

- **Whether you are on the field or on the bench, be the best teammate possible.** Cheer on your fellow players, root for the team's success, and celebrate goals and excellent plays and bring positivity to mistakes.

Communicating with Refs, Teammates, and Parents Don'ts

- **Don't fight with your own teammates on the field.** This looks bad, and it is not going to result in either of you playing better. You are on the *same team!* Act like it!

- **Don't argue with a ref on a call.** There is zero percent chance you are going to change their mind, and you're only making it worse for yourself and the team. If there is an opponent on the other team who keeps tugging on your jersey or you are noticing the offside is questionable many times during the first half, calmly speak to the ref one-on-one and make them aware of your concern. They will appreciate this way more, and chances are there will be a call in the second half reflecting it!

- **Always treat your parents with respect, whether or not you want to take their advice.** They have been on this crazy soccer journey with you and they only have the best intentions, so if you had a bad game and don't feel like hearing them tell you what you did right or wrong, be polite about it! Express to them you need time to decompress and will chat with them later about how you felt about the game.

- **Don't sulk when you're not on the field.** Coaches have eyes like a hawk (in the backs of their heads, too), and the best way to stay on that bench permanently is to sulk and not support your teammate.

- **Don't talk back to a coach.** This is a big no-no. If you have a major issue with something a coach says or does, instead of talking back, calmly and politely schedule a meeting with them after that game or practice. (Let's be honest, it's very easy to be a raging lunatic after a game.) After you've taken the time to calm down, write down your thoughts in a clear way and walk into the meeting ready to speak about the issue in a mature manner.

  - Shannon remembers having a disagreement with her coach during practice after the beep test, and being in the heat of the moment didn't lead to anything positive! (Cue being benched the next game.) Instead, wait until you have collected your thoughts and address the situation in a better manner!

Chapter Thirteen

OFFSEASON

Offseason (*noun*): LOL. JK. It's a myth. Please see the definition for "in season."

The offseason is a time of year when you aren't playing conference games, but you are still juggling practice, lifting, fitness, classes, a social life, and more. Sometimes "offseason" can be just as hard as in-season, if not harder, because this is when you don't need to save your legs for game day. It's time to build and grow to get better for next season. Chances are your fitness sessions and lifts are more challenging during this time of year. The positive is you aren't spending a ton of time traveling to away games, but your schedule is still jam-packed. So what we are trying to say is there really is *no* such thing as an "offseason," but you are going to find that keeping a schedule and having time management skills will help you to get better during this period.

Offseason Dos

- **Be prepared to work out during the offseason.** There is a chance your coach will focus *even more* on keeping your team in shape and getting stronger, now that you

OFF SEASON

don't have weekly conference games to stay rested for. It may differ depending on the division you are in, but we personally had conditioning six days a week at 6:00 AM and team lifts twice a week. After all, if you haven't noticed, there really is no offseason. You'll always have to be on.

SoccerGirlProblems®
@SoccerGrlProbs

When coach says you have the DAY OFF but you're like...yeahhhhh what's the catch? #SoccerGrlProbs #NODaysOff

- **Let go of the mental stress of being in-season.** Let loose! Live a little! Stay up past your bedtime! Catch up on that season of *Riverdale* or *Keeping up with Kardashians* you've missed every episode of because you've been too tired at night to stay up and watch it. And *yes*, socialize (responsibly and safely) with your friends, both team and non-team friends.

- **Focus on your individual game.** If you're in college, NCAA rules set limitations on the amount of hours your coach can schedule. Your time spent practicing with your team will consist of fewer hours in the offseason, so this is your time to work on your individual game (e.g., footwork, first touch, juggling, etc.). However, be prepared that some coaches will find loopholes in this with "captain's practices" and "optional" lifts. (Every school and team will be different with this.) And, FYI, usually when something is "optional" it's actually mandatory. AKA, Coach will notice if you don't do it.

155

CREDIT: Keara Russell

- **Take the classes you weren't able to fit in during your regular season semester!** Now is the time to add more to your course load if you weren't able to before!

- **Fear not; just because it's not a game day doesn't mean you can't wear your favorite game day sweats!** That team gear is *comfy.*

Offseason Don'ts

- **Don't get out of shape.** While you should be giving your body a healthy rest after such a long season, you shouldn't be resting with reckless abandon. Going out and partying, overeating, barely training, and letting your offseason workout packet collect dust will undo all of that progress you made during the season. Enjoy yourself with friends, but keep your priorities in mind. That winter training is just around the corner!

- **What your coach expects:** running, recovering, technical training, mental preparation.

- **What you should do:** running, recovering, technical training, mental preparation.

- **What we actually do:** lie down, nap, eat, watch TV, think about working out.

• **Don't go wild.** You're going to want to go wild. But just trust us and don't get *too* wild. Yes, if you are of legal drinking age in college, this is your time to responsibly socialize with others in a bar setting if you choose to do so. Just keep in mind that you are still a representation of your school's athletic department and your team. In addition to that, your body and what you put into your body is that much more important when you are an athlete. You've put a lot of work into your physical fitness. Don't throw it all away by treating your body like garbage. Take-home message: don't be stupid.

• **Don't think the offseason games don't matter.** If you are a starting player, this is your time to assure your coach that you deserve to be a starting player for next season. If you are a substitute who didn't get much time during the conference games, this is your chance to show your coach that you deserve more playing time. Even though these games don't matter...they matter.

Chapter Fourteen

RECRUITING AND PLAYING AT THE NEXT LEVEL

Recruiting (*verb*): The act of emails and/or in-person stalking by a college coach in an attempt to seek out the most dedicated and hardworking of the Ladyballers. They do this in hopes of adopting them to the lovable band of misfits known as his team. Said coach may even pay you a big chunk of moolah to commit to his team.

Recruiting is to many Ladyballers the *most* nerve-racking time of their soccer career. How do you reach out to college coaches? What do you say when you reach out to them? How many coaches should you email and how serious should you be about the school? What should you do to stand out when they come to watch you play? How do you not get nervous when they come watch you play? It's *stressful!* Believe us, we have each been there and we were stressed to the *max* from it. At the time, we each wished there were more information available on the recruiting process. It wasn't like we were the first to go through it; literally thousands of players had

CREDIT: Keara Russell

done this before us. Well...fear not, we broke down everything we've learned about the process so you won't be as in the dark about it all as we were! Now you have the tools to get through the recruiting process as smoothly and stress-free as possible (okay, stress-free, that's a stretch—but you won't be as stressed as we were!).

Research and Communication Dos

- **Contact the coach in a responsible manner.** Spell his or her name and the school name correctly, and show that you have done your research. A well-thought-out email can show Coach that you are a mature individual who can handle the academic and athletic workload. Let them know that you have what it takes to become an NCAA student-athlete...emphasis on *student*.

- **Familiarize yourself with the differences between Division I, II, and III.** Division I and II, for example, can award athletic scholarships to their incoming athletes, while Division III does not. Academic scholarships are possible at all three Divisions, though! The NCAA has rules and regulations for the numbers of hours of commitment each Division is allowed to require of its athletes in season and out of season. Division I is permitted more hours of play per week than Division II and Division III. These are just some of the differences between Divisions, and you can read more on the NCAA website. Definitely take these differences into account when searching for your perfect school!

- **Make sure that you are not only researching the school's website, but also the *athletic* website.** Check out the team roster. Familiarize yourself with how many girls are on the team. How many freshmen? How well did they do last season? What conference are they in? Who has the most hilarious action shots? (We're kidding, but they always seem to pick the worst ones.) This knowledge will set you apart from the average recruit, and your email has a better chance of getting read as a result. You will look more interested, passionate, and invested—period. There's no such thing as being too prepared.

- **Put your name in the subject line of the email. Coaches receive hundreds of recruiting emails.** It can be very hard for them to remember everyone who has contacted them. Putting your name in the subject line means it is right in front of their face, giving you better odds of having your name stand out.

- **In this day and age, there are endless ways to watch games.** On TV, streaming, on social media—take advantage of it! Watch the games of the team you're interested in: What formation do they play? What position are you? Can you picture yourself being on that field? Can you picture yourself fitting into their style of play? If not, are you willing to make an effort? Are you coachable? Would you consider playing other positions? (Versatility is one of the most valued attributes, so we are answering this for you: **Y-E-S**. You will play any position needed...unless you're a goalkeeper, and even then you're flexible.) Pick the coach's brain about this. Actually, pick the coach's brain about any of the aforementioned topics. Most of your peers won't be comparing and contrasting standard and diamond-midfield 4-4-2 formations. These sorts of questions are imperative; you don't want to end up on a team that doesn't utilize outside mids when your best asset is low-lined crosses from the wing during the run of play. But then again, maybe

CREDIT: Keara Russell

you're such a baller that you can adjust and your skill set can be fully utilized. *Ask!*

- **Pick a school that has multiple majors that interest you.** At most schools, you don't have to declare a major until halfway through sophomore year, so you'll want to take classes in a variety of subjects. The majority of college freshmen aren't set on a career, but if you are, don't settle for a school that doesn't have what you want. There are literally hundreds of schools at each division, so there will be one that's the perfect fit for you! That being said, you'll be surprised what classes and subjects you find interesting! Keep an open mind, because you're about to experience a lot of change over this four-year adventure we call college.

Research and Communication Don'ts

- **Don't email your potential college's coach with an email address that starts with xoxSoccerBabixox or IKickBalls.** If you don't already have one, make sure you create an appropriate email address. The more generic, the better. Keep it simple—for example, FirstNameLastName@ domain.com. We've heard from coaches that they feel you are way less credible as a potential recruit when you email them with an immature email address. Also please DO NOT have your parents email them! That is a big no! If you are old enough to play college soccer, you are old enough to email them on your own!

- **Manners and professionalism are key in emails.** It's the first impression you'll make on a potential coach. A "YO COACH," with the following, all-too-typical, "I'd love to play soccer for your school," is a one-way ticket to the trash bin.

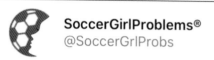

SoccerGirlProblems®
@SoccerGrlProbs

If your email doesn't have your jersey number or lucky number in it, are you even an athlete? #SoccerGrlProbs

It's immediately obvious when it was a cut-and-paste-to-15-coaches job. Be creative; we don't adorn just *anyone* with the Ladyballer moniker. Earn that title and show your potential coach why you are one. Ask a teammate who has gone through the recruiting process to check your email and see if they have any tips!

- **Don't misspell any words or make blatant grammatical errors.** Double- and triple-check everything, from your email signature to the correct usage of your/you're. You'd be shocked to know (and around practice you *will* hear about) how many potential recruits get tossed into the trash bin because of a sentence like, "Ur school is at the top of my list." This isn't a text message; grammar and spelling matter. And while we're on the topic, don't be that girl who tries to email Alabama State but writes Notre Dame instead. 😬 This is where you can ask your parents for help, also known as Dictionary Dad and Master of Words Mom.

Visit Schools Dos

- **Once you narrow down your search to five or six schools, physically visit each one.** Bear in mind you're not going there *just* to play soccer (academics and community are important, ya'll). We promise you this: stepping foot on campus will make or break your decision. Don't be stubborn or lazy. What's one more weekend dedicated to soccer, right? Pack up the car with Mom or Dad and maybe even drag a BFF or two with you; NARPs need to see schools, too! Fairfield University's town life, campus feel, classroom size, and soccer team, as well as the facilities (and most

CREDIT: Abby Lydey

importantly, the cafeteria), are what won us over on our visits. Seeing our school really made an impact on our decision to go there. If we didn't physically get our butts to campus, SoccerGrlProbs would likely never have come into being. So, like Nike, *just do it!*

- Shannon remembers wanting to go far away to college, but she kept an open mind and once she saw Fairfield in person she knew it was the perfect fit for her! Seeing the school in person is a lot different than what you see online, so definitely make this a priority!

• **If you have an official visit or on-campus visit to the school, ask *everything* you want to know.** There's no such thing as a stupid question. While your parents may have a minivan's worth of questions, at the end of the day, *you're* the one going to the school. The girls on the team will have the best (read: most honest) answers for you because they are currently at the school. They know which dorms get the hottest in the summer, which days to avoid the cafeteria food, the best time of day to head to the gym, and what professors and classes to take. You don't want to get stuck taking World Literature 101 with a teacher who has a well-established issue with athletes missing class for away games. If you don't have one scheduled, don't let that stop you from walking around campus and checking things out for yourself.

• **When you're on campus, check out all the dorms, from freshman to senior housing.** Grab a coffee (or burrito, if you're feeling crazy) at the cafeteria, go to the library, walk through the campus center, check out the bulletin boards for the school activities that week. You'll get a good feel for a school's energy this way. You're also choosing a culture when you decide on a school!

- **Sit in on a class and see how you like it.** Schools vary in class size; bigger schools can have lecture halls with hundreds of students, while some smaller universities pride themselves on a quality student-to-teacher ratio with 10 to 20 students per class. Make sure you go with what works best with your learning style. Personally, we loved that Fairfield University had smaller classes because the relationship between teachers and students was much more personal.

  - ■ **Tip:** If your teacher knows you well, chances are you won't be just another name on the attendance sheet. You'll pay attention more, be more engaged with your classes, and the chances are higher that a professor will be more likely to write you that coveted recommendation for graduate school or highly competitive job opportunity when the time comes.

CREDIT: Keara Russell

Visit Schools Don'ts

- **Don't just care about how good the soccer team is in the conference.** Make sure you that you research both the athletic and academic side of things. Unless you plan on being a professional soccer player (and hey, maybe you will be), there is a good chance your future career will likely not include a ball and cleats. If all goes well, you'll graduate from your future school in four years. What are you going to do afterward? You guessed it: work! Unfortunately, only Peter Pan stays young forever. One day, you'll get a job and join the real world. Make sure you're academically fit for that school so that you set yourself up for success in the classroom and life after school.

- **Don't ignore the academic questions!** Ask yourself: *Do they offer the major I'm interested in? Does the athletic center make their student-athletes' academics a priority? Are there private tutors? Does the coach allow nursing majors? Engineers? Can I balance the school/sports workload with a major that requires 20-plus hours of extraneous work per week? What is the minimum GPA to be able to play? What is the expected GPA of the team?* All of these questions are vital to where you'll ultimately end up. If you find you can't answer some of these (or that the answers you'd hoped for didn't pop up), ask someone! You don't want to report to preseason in the brutal August heat, find out you hate it, and transfer later on.

  - We know the prospect of choosing your future is extremely overwhelming, but we promise it's not nearly as daunting as you've been told. If you get started early, voice your feelings as they come, and are open and honest (with yourself and your family) about what you want, it will be a breeze. Your transition to college will be as smooth and painless as you imagined it. Hang in there, girlfriend!

Get to Know the Team and the Coach Dos

- **When you have a scheduled visit to the school, catch one of the team's home games.** It's imperative to get a feel for the team in their most natural setting. How does the coach behave during games? How does the team react when a goal is scored? Even more important: How does a team react when they concede a goal? What is the fan atmosphere like? Sometimes the coach will let you speak with the players after and shadow them for the day. It helps you get a better idea of what you like and don't like. Let's face it, girl; you're going to be in that locker room and with those teammates *a lot*!

- **Put yourself out there!** You are already a crazy soccer girl with 18 crazy soccer friends. Don't be afraid to direct message a girl on the team on Facebook or Instagram if

CREDIT: Abby Lydey

you're serious about the school. (It's not weird, we promise!) Don't shy away from picking up the phone and calling the coach who hasn't had the time to get back to you. They will take note of how interested and passionate you are about the school if you follow up. Truth be told, in all aspects of life, persistence is key. If you are shy and quiet, that's okay! But for recruiting, try to let the coach see the more comfortable, confident side of you. Remember that coaches are, first and foremost, people, too. Don't psych yourself out. Their veins run red with blood just like yours do; treat them as you would any other adult (and by that, we mean respectfully).

- **Let the coach and team get to know *you*, too!** You are one of dozens of recruits the coach will be introducing to the team. How are you going to make yourself stand out? Be you. As Oscar Wilde is believed to have said, "Be yourself; everyone else is already taken."

Get to Know the Team and Coach Don'ts

- **Don't let the team and coach get the wrong impression of you from your social media!** Be smart about this. Does your coach want to see pictures of you being irresponsible with your friends or a bunch of "sexy selfies?" *No!* College coaches are sifting through hundreds of potential recruits, carefully choosing young women who represent the program they have worked tirelessly to improve. Do they want to see that you're family-oriented and value the important relationships in your life? *Yes!* Today, social media profiles are your first impression on people, often before you've met them. And trust us, the coaches and athletic department *will* look at social media. Don't let them think

CREDIT: Keara Russell

poorly of you. You can make your accounts private, but odds are someone from the school will follow you so be ruthlessly careful about what you post.

- **Don't partake in activities that you don't feel comfortable doing.** If you are visiting a school and some of the players go out drinking, ***do not*** *feel pressured to join!* You are visiting the school to make a good impression on the coach and the team. The last thing you need is the coach cutting off communication or rescinding an offer because you went along with an activity you shouldn't have been a part of. We've seen this happen with potential recruits. Silly mistakes can not only derail your career, but they can dictate your future. Be social, be energetic, but above all things, be smart. If anyone tells you that you *must* drink to fit in, feel free to head back to the dorm. It us up to *you* to dictate when you're good and ready to engage in those sorts of activities...no one else. Being smart doesn't only have to apply to drinking. On campus, all eyes are on student-athletes; what you say and what you do has a bigger impact on the university than the average student. Even if you're not partaking in anything illegal, it's in your best interest to represent the school and the program at all times.

Weigh Your Options Dos

- **Make pro/con lists.** As cheesy as this sounds, they're undervalued! It may sound like a pain in the butt, and something that your mom would nag you about, but do it. We promise that you'll have epiphanies over the smallest points, and it may help you narrow down your search. Plus, apparently, crossing things off lists releases endorphins and puts you in a better mood, so go get pen-happy! You have all that time during rides to practice, games, and away tournaments. Utilize it!

- **Apply for scholarships, grants, and financial aid.** At the Division I level, only a portion of student-athletes receive some sort of athletic financial aid. This is especially low when you consider how many foreign players come to the U.S. with scholarships. Keep in mind, as the Division goes to II and III, there is even less funding for scholarships. Life is expensive, and so is college tuition. While it would be great for everyone to get full athletic scholarships, most schools won't have more than a handful of these for their team. If a team can only give seven scholarships, for example, this could either be given to seven different girls or it could be split up into half and quarter-scholarships so that more athletes can benefit. If you're exceptional academically, you should apply for an academic scholarship, because this could make up the difference for the money you weren't able to get athletically. So, think outside the box and apply for academic scholarships, grants, and financial aid. Your family—and your future bank account—will be endlessly grateful. The hours it will take you to research and apply for these is well worth it. Talk to your guidance counselor for help. That's why they're there!

Weigh Your Options Don'ts

- **Don't get overwhelmed and pick the easiest choice to avoid the stress.** We all decided on Fairfield University, but only after carefully weighing all of our options, making numerous pro/con lists, meeting the coaches, going on visits, and talking at length with the girls on the team. At the end of the day, Fairfield just happened to be the right place for all of us, for some reasons that are similar, and some vastly different. This is one of the more important decisions in your life...don't shortchange yourself by going through the process halfheartedly.

- **Don't pick a school based on where your friends/ significant other are going!** Make the choice that's right for you. (We know from personal experience that friends and significant others can change from high school to college.) Besides, there will be that many more colleges you can go and visit (insert salsa dancing emoji here).

- **Don't feel pressured by family or anyone else to go to a school because that's what *they* want you to do.** You can value their opinion, but still make your own choice for what's best for you. Also, don't feel pressured just because a relative went to a specific school and they want you to carry the tradition. What worked best for them may not work best for you.

Our Stories

At the end of the day, every single player you talk to will have a different story about how she was recruited and why she chose the school that she did. Each of us SoccerGrlProbs ladies had a different experience, ones we wanted to tell you about in our own words.

PHOTO CREDIT: Marwan Shousher

Name: Carly Beyar

Position: No. 17, forward; recruited as center back, transitioned to outside mid and forward

Major: Communications (although I should have majored in Business); Studio Art minor

During my sophomore and junior years of high school I played for Alberstson Fury and the OAP program, where we attended a ton of college showcases. I was being recruited by various schools including Providence, University of Connecticut, and University of Virginia. Although I visited other colleges, I did an overnight visit at those three to get a better feel of how I liked the atmosphere and the experience—and *boy* was I happy I did. The visits helped me truly grasp how my college career would turn out if I committed to that particular school.

It wasn't until the end of my sophomore year when I was at my travel team indoor tournament that it hit me: I noticed my coach was speaking to a tall man on the sideline while we were playing small-sided (and I have to admit, this guy came on the right day). I was firing shots on frame, working my absolute hardest to win the ball back, challenging defenders 1v1 to goal. It was one of my best games. It turned out that the tall, tan guy was the Fairfield University women's soccer head coach, and he had come to my game to see our goalkeeper. Afterward, he ended up wanting to recruit *me*, too! I immediately set up a visit.

When I drove into the town of Fairfield, I fell in love with it. The campus is close to the beach; the town was adorable and filled with interesting family-owned shops and unique restaurants. On campus, the all-grass soccer field and athletic facilities were amazing. I had a gut feeling that Fairfield was the school for me. At the end of the day, here are my takeaways:

Research. I could compare Fairfield to all of the various other schools I'd visited.

Visualize. Picture a day in the life at that school. How long does it take to get from class to practice? Are you walking everywhere or taking a shuttle? How do you feel in a specific-size class?

Make pro/con lists. It was easy for me to see that Fairfield had all the pros. I ended up verbally committing early in my junior year of high school, and the rest is history.

Name: Shannon Fay

Position: No. 22, forward

Major: Communications; Psychology and Film & Television Minors

I was convinced I would go to school far, far away from my home on Long Island, New York. I wanted to go to school in California, North Carolina, or Florida, so I began emailing and contacting college coaches in those states. My mom told me to be more open to other geographic locations; she said, "You never know what school you may end up falling in love with." I started early, going with my brother to check out different schools and reading about them online and in college books. I went on a ton of unofficial visits, official visits, and tours of different colleges throughout the country. I made pro/con lists 'til my fingers hurt, emailed coaches of schools I liked, and went to college showcases all over. My first choice was originally Elon University and, of course, every game the coach came to I played *awful*. #SoccerGrlProbs. I got so nervous about playing well, I would end up playing worse because of my anxiety.

If I could give you some advice, it would be as follows:

Don't forget why you started playing this game. You love this game, and you should always play for the love of the game. Playing scared or nervous because of the pressure of a teammate, parent, coach, or recruiter is no way to live.

Be confident in your ability and play the game the way you always do no matter who is watching. Once I finally began to play with less fear at recruiting tournaments and camps, there was more interest from college programs. My junior year seemed like one long recruiting process, and I eventually found my perfect fit no farther than two hours from my hometown. Fairfield University had everything on my list. I wanted a small school with a college-town vibe, classes with 20 or fewer students so I could get more face time with the professors, a beautiful campus that was walkable, and a team and coach I felt I would mesh well with. It wasn't in Florida or California, but that didn't matter!

Keeping my options open and being open-minded was the best thing I could have done, and I'm so grateful I didn't close the door on the opportunity to play for and attend Fairfield University—without it, I wouldn't be where I am today.

Name: Alanna Locast

Position: No. 13, forward

Major: Exercise Physiology Masters: Biology

My recruiting story was a bit of an unconventional one. I was so sure at the end of my senior year of high school that I wanted to be a regular college student (a NARP). I had been a little burnt out from playing 12 seasons in high school throughout three different sports, in addition to travel teams, and I thought to myself, *I'd love to see what it's like to be a normal college student and just have to focus on my school work. I can play club soccer for fun, right? That will be enough.* So I ended all contact with coaches and applied to Fairfield University, purely for academic purposes.

A semester into college, I found myself miserable and like a sad lost puppy without soccer in my life. I desperately needed the competition and challenge and team environment that I was so badly missing in my life. Club soccer just wasn't cutting it for me. I felt like I was suffocating just taking classes and having no outlet or stress-relieving time in a sport. So I looked up the soccer coach's email address and nervously wrote him a lengthy, formal email explaining why I wanted to play for his team and begging him to meet me. He had me come to his office the following day. I walked in a nervous wreck, sat down, and told him how badly I wanted to play at the next level, how much I missed pushing myself, and how I thought I could contribute to his team. The University didn't hold tryouts, so what my coach did instead was allow me to attend the team camp over the summer.

One day of camp. That was all I had to show everything I possibly could about me as a player and leader and teammate. No pressure at all, right? I went to that one day of camp a trembling, horrified ball of nerves and ran my head off. I think it was my work ethic that won him over and convinced him to give me a shot on the team. It was one of the best decisions I've ever made, and I owe a big thank you to my coach for seeing something in me worth giving a chance.

Epilogue

FAST-FORWARD TO SENIOR YEAR

In the blink of the eye, you're here. Your last game, senior game. It's (hopefully) the championship, if your team has gone far enough. Four years seemed to sprint by faster than that deadly mile test you're forced to run every preseason. Four years of blood, sweat, and tears have all come down to that final game of the season. Here you stand, in the locker room that has become your second home, lacing up the duct-taped cleats that are fraying at the soles, the ones that have never let you down. Slide those protective shin guards into your grass-stained socks with rips at the ankles.

At one point or another you may have been lost, lonely, and scared. You may have been stumbling into that locker room not knowing where you belong. You were nowhere near the strong, resilient leader you now see in the mirror. In this moment, you reflect back on everything: the journey that brought you here is now clearer than ever. The long hours, the exhausting practices, the extra technical sessions under the hot sun were worth it because it got you to where you are now. You've long accepted always being sore, knowing the pain will breed stronger tomorrows. The lone wolf you once were is now part of the wolf pack you call family. You've realized you can achieve far more as a fearless team than you ever could as an individual. You've learned that your strongest muscle is your heart, and you speak with your feet—the loudest voice you have. Battles have been won and lost, but you've learned to leave everything you have out on the field always. Effort, desire, heart, hustle—life is about earning your reputation and demanding respect. Ninety minutes is the time you've learned to love seeing up on the scoreboard because each game is a new beginning, another chance to prove your

DO YOU REMEMBER WHY YOU PLAY OR HAS IT BEEN TOO LONG? IS IT BECAUS YOU'VE WORKED SO HARD TO GET WHERE YOU ARE, OR BECAUSE YOU LOVE TO BE PART OF A TEAM? IS IT BECAUSE YOU LOVE THE ROAR OF THE CROWD, OR THE ANXIETY BEFORE THE GAME? IS IT BECAUSE YOU DON'T WANT TO LET ANYONE DOWN, OR YOURSELF? IS IT BECAUSE YOU LOVE THE SOUND OF THE PERFECT GOAL, OR BECAUSE YOU'D RATHER BE ON THE FIELD THAN ANYWHERE ELSE IN THE WORLD? SOMEWHERE BEHIND THE ATHLETE YOU'VE BECOME AND THE HOURS OF PRACTICE, AND THE COACHES WHO PUSHED YOU AND THE TEAMMATES WHO BELIEVED IN YOU AND THE FANS WHO CHEERED FOR YOU, IS THE LITTLE GIRL WHO SHOT THE BALL, MADE THE SAVE— THE ONE WHO FELL IN LOVE WITH THE GAME AND NEVER LOOKED BACK. PLAY FOR HER!

worth. You've grown to love the game more than you ever thought possible, and you wouldn't trade it for anything.

You're out on the field, staring up at the scoreboard. Ninety minutes on the clock. An avalanche of adrenaline courses through your veins the moment you step out there. You see your name up on a sign, one your family and friends adorned for you, the same people that traveled all this way to see you play one final match.

You've got your 20-something best friends beside you. You stare down at the jersey you've worn for nearly half a decade now and swell with pride as you realize it's the last time you'll put it on. You've survived four of the most demanding but rewarding years of your life. You haven't just survived, you've thrived. This is your last chance to prove your worth. The referee blows the whistle. The clock begins. Your teammate taps the ball to you. You don't think…you just go.

"Do you remember why you play or has it been too long? Is it because you've worked so hard to get where you are, or because you love to be part of a team? Is it because you love the roar of the crowd, or the anxiety before the game? Is it because you don't want to let anyone down or yourself? Is it because you love the sound of the perfect goal, or because you'd rather be on the field than anywhere else in the world? Somewhere behind the athlete you've become and the hours of practice, and the coaches who pushed you, and the teammates who believed in you and the fans who cheered for you, is the little girl who shot the ball, made the save—the one who fell in love with the game and never looked back. Play for her!"

—Mia Hamm

CREDIT: Keara Russell

50 THINGS I WISH I KNEW BEFORE PLAYING COLLEGE SOCCER

1. Don't be late. Ever. The whole team will pay for it.

2. Bright underwear on the day of a home game (white shorts) is never a good idea.

3. On-sale sports bras. Take advantage of deals like this.

4. Listen to the advice your parents give you after games. Whether they're right or wrong, this is how they show you they love you.

5. You don't need flashy cleats. Your footwork will speak for itself.

6. Some people will never see your potential; don't let it stop you from trying.

7. Always share your pre-wrap. You'll need to borrow someone's someday.

8. Being skinnier does not mean you're a better athlete or faster.

9. There is more to life than missing a party.

10. Respect your seniors and "play for them." You'll be there one day.

11. Be kind to the freshmen. You were there at one point, and it sucks just as much for them as it did for you.

12. Always drink water when your coach gives you a water break, whether you're thirsty or not.

13. Your bruises and scars are something to be proud of, not hide.

14. Bring an external charger on the bus. The outlets never work.

15. Keep your locker clean. Trust us on this one.

16. Never blame yourself for losing in penalty kicks. It never should have been tied in the first place.

17. Double up your sports bra for extra support.

18. Take it easy with the makeup before games.

19. Intensity is beautiful. Don't ever let anyone make you feel bad for trying too hard.

20. If they try to bring you down, say goodbye.

21. Stop venting your problems out loud. Your coaches and teammates won't appreciate the negativity.

22. Be nice to your parents after your game, no matter how angry you are that you lost.

23. Take your classes seriously.

24. Eat more and take care of yourself. With hours of practice and games, your body needs more fuel. Listen to it.

25. It doesn't matter how thick you think lifting is making you; don't avoid weights.

26. Going out on the weekends is all fun and games until you're up at 6:00 AM on a Monday for conditioning.

27. You can be great without being a starter.

28. Don't pretend for a second to be someone you are not just to impress people. You'll lose yourself.

29. Write down your goals.

30. Kill them with kindness.

31. Don't assign blame. Maybe that free kick wasn't your fault, but making somebody else feel like it was their fault is only hurting the team.

32. If he or she can't understand your busy schedule, they probably never will.

33. It's one bad practice. Don't let it carry over into your next one.

34. Embrace Panera. It will seem like a Thanksgiving meal compared to the Subway sandwich you get every time you travel.

35. No matter how oblivious your coach acts, he knows all the latest gossip.

36. Your mom knows when you're hurting well before you'll admit it to yourself.

37. Who cares if you have bad tan lines in the summer? Wear shorts anyway.

38. Throw your hair up in a soaking wet bun and don't think twice about it. You won't have time to perfectly straighten it.

39. Act with class, always. Your coach has eyes and ears everywhere, and you're a representation of your team.

40. Keep your composure. Flipping out at practice or a game never helped any situation.

41. Talk with respect to your coach, teammates, and referees. Being rude won't get you anywhere.

42. High school years are not the best years of your life.

43. Your senior game will be sad, but smile for your family anyway.

44. Don't get annoyed by a teammate who follows you around. Imitation is a form of flattery.

45. You can still be a good teammate without needing to be best friends with somebody.

46. Don't hesitate to tell a teammate something you admire about her. You never know what it could mean to her.

47. Don't walk on the concrete with your brand-new cleats. You'll regret it.

48. Get good at putting on your socks and shin guards and cleats really fast. Rushing will inevitably happen.

49. Even if you're the most fit person on your team, conditioning isn't "stupid." It's about your team going through something together.

50. Eat the damn donut.

Acknowledgments

We are proud to say that SoccerGrlProbs is a product of community and we are so incredibly grateful for everyone in our big "soccer family." From fellow Ladyballers and their families who have supported us on social media and in emails to the long list of coaches, mentors, alumni, and even kind strangers who have helped us along the way, we have been able to take this company as far as we have because of community.

Thank you to our teammates and coaches, Sean and Jim, who helped us spark the creation of this one-of a-kind soccer family. Without you, there would be no hilarious videos or soccer problems to tweet about. You are more than just a team. You are family. #GoStags

Thank you to our mentors, who selflessly dedicated their time, help, and resources without expecting anything in return. Chris Huntley, Michael McDonald, Teddy Spicer, and Ed Kelly; we have come to you over the years with every question imaginable about our business. You have always kept your doors open and offered advice without hesitation, providing us a great sense of security as we navigated the ins and outs of starting our own company.

Thank you to our parents, siblings, and friends for letting us fill your garages and basements with apparel, for literally folding and packaging shirts into the night with us, and for being our lifelines from the beginning as we were figuring this whole "business thing" out! Knowing that you undeniably had our backs helped us to proudly and confidently tackle the obstacles we faced.

Thank you to all our soccer idols who paved the way for women's soccer when the path did not yet exist. You gave us an image of strong, confident, and resilient females that we could aspire to when we were growing up. Mia Hamm, Kristine Lilly, Brandi Chastain, Julie Foudy, Michelle Akers, Abby Wambach, and the rest of the brilliantly talented and beautifully strong USWNT players, you helped give us the courage to use our platform to further unite and inspire Ladyballers everywhere.

And last but not least, thank you to Fairfield University, for being the home away from home that brought us together at the start of it all...